ALEKSANDR BLOK'S TRILOGY OF LYRIC DRAMAS

Aleksandr Blok's Trilogy of Lyric Dramas gathers together for the first time in English translation the first three plays by Aleksandr Blok, the pre-eminent poet of Russian Symbolism and one of the greatest poets of the twentieth century. The three plays that constitute the trilogy – *A Puppet Show, The King on the Square* and *The Unknown Woman* – are pivotal documents in the development of modernist drama.

In his productions of *A Puppet Show* and *The Unknown Woman*, Meyerhold first began to work out the basic tenets of his approach to grotesque and constructivist theatre. Moreover, *A Puppet Show* provided the inspiration and much of the foundation for Meyerhold's theoretical writings. As a result, these plays are indispensable to any student of Meyerhold or modernist theatre. The plays are presented in the context of the poetry from which they issued in order to suggest how Blok developed the themes and motifs of the plays in other genres.

Timothy C. Westphalen graduated *magna cum laude* from Knox College, and went on to earn an M.A. and a Ph.D. in Slavic Languages and Literatures from Harvard University. He has published in leading academic journals and has received awards for excellence in teaching. He is currently an Associate Professor at the State University of New York at Stony Brook.

Russian Theatre Archive

A series of books edited by John Freedman

Volume 1
The Major Plays of Nikolai Erdman
translated and edited by John Freedman

Volume 2
A Meeting About Laughter
Sketches, Interludes and Theatrical Parodies by Nikolai Erdman
with Vladimir Mass and Others
translated and edited by John Freedman

Volume 3
Theatre in the Solovki Prison Camp
Natalia Kuziakina

Volume 4
Sergei Radlov: The Shakespearian Fate of a Soviet Director
David Zolotnitsky

Volume 5
Bulgakov: The Novelist–Playwright
edited by Lesley Milne

Volume 6
Aleksandr Vampilov: The Major Plays
translated and edited by Alma Law

Volume 7
The Death of Tarelkin and Other Plays:
The Trilogy of Alexander Sukhovo-Kobylin
translated and edited by Harold B. Segel

Volume 8
A Chekhov Quartet
translated and adapted by Vera Gottlieb

Volume 9
Two Plays from the New Russia
Bald/Brunet by Daniil Gink and *Nijinsky* by Alexei Burykin
translated and edited by John Freedman

Volume 10
Russian Comedy of the Nikolaian Era
translated and with an introduction by Laurence Senelick

Volume 11
Meyerhold Speaks/Meyerhold Rehearses
by Aleksandr Gladkov
translated, edited and with an introduction by Alma Law

Volume 12
Moscow Performances:
The New Russian Theater 1991–1996
John Freedman

Volume 13
Lyric Incarnate:
The Dramas of Aleksandr Blok
Timothy C. Westphalen

Volume 14
Russian Mirror:
Three Plays by Russian Women
edited by Melissa Smith

Volume 15
Two Comedies by Catherine the Great, Empress of Russia:
Oh, These Times! and *The Siberian Shaman*
translated and edited by Lurana Donnels O'Malley

Volume 16
Off Nevsky Prospect:
St Petersburg's Theatre Studios in the 1980s and 1990s
Elena Markova

Volume 17
Stanislavsky in Focus
Sharon Marie Carnicke

Volume 18
Two Plays by Olga Mukhina
translated and edited by John Freedman

Volume 19
The Simpleton
by Sergei Kokovkin
translated and edited by John Freedman

Volume 20
Moscow Performances II:
The 1996–1997 Season
John Freedman

Volume 21
Your Murderer
by Vassily Aksyonov
translated by Daniel Gerould and Jadwiga Kosicka,
with an introduction by Daniel Gerould

Volume 22
Aleksandr Blok's Trilogy of Lyric Dramas:
A Puppet Show, The King on the Square
and *The Unknown Woman*
translated and edited by Timothy C. Westphalen

ALEKSANDR BLOK'S TRILOGY OF LYRIC DRAMAS

A Puppet Show, *The King on the Square* and *The Unknown Woman*

Translated and edited by
Timothy C. Westphalen

LONDON AND NEW YORK

First published 2003
by Routledge
2 Park Square, Milton Park, Abingdon, Oxfordshire OX14 4RN

Simultaneously published in the USA and Canada
by Routledge
711 Third Avenue, New York, NY 10017

First issued in paperback 2014

Routledge is an imprint of the Taylor and Francis Group, an informa company

© 2003 Taylor & Francis

Typeset in Stempel Garamond by M Rules

All rights reserved. No part of this book may be reprinted or reproduced or utilised in any form or by any electronic, mechanical, or other means, now known or hereafter invented, including photocopying and recording, or in any information storage or retrieval system, without permission in writing from the publishers.

British Library Cataloguing in Publication Data
A catalogue record for this book is available from the British Library

Library of Congress Cataloging in Publication Data
A catalog record for this book has been requested

ISBN 978-0-415-28050-1 (hbk)
ISBN 978-0-415-75383-8 (pbk)

CONTENTS

List of plates	ix
Introduction to the series	xi
Introduction: Exit from lyric isolation	1
A PUPPET SHOW	19
Context of *A Puppet Show*: related poems	35
A puppet show	35
Light staggered in the window	36
He showed up at a well-ordered ball	37
At round tables, everybody was screaming	38
You will dress me in silver	39
At that hour when narcissuses are getting drunk	40
A travelling show	41
THE KING ON THE SQUARE	43
Context of *The King on the Square*	75
Her coming	75
Of love, poetry, and government service	82
THE UNKNOWN WOMAN	91
Context of *The Unknown Woman*: related poems	121
The unknown woman	121
There, in the hard, howling frost of the night	123
Star-strewn train	124
Your face is paler than it was	125
There ladies flaunt fashions	127

LIST OF PLATES

1 Aleksandr Blok in 1891–92   x
2 Aleksandr Blok in 1911   xii
3 A poster for the production of *The Unknown Woman* and *A Puppet Show* by Vsevolod Meyerhold at the Tenishevsky school auditorium in 1914   34
4 Fomin's sketch for costumes for a production of *A Puppet Show* in Petrograd, 1920   42
5 Lentulov's sketch for the Redheaded Gentleman from *The Unknown Woman*, Moscow 1918   102
6 Lentulov's sketch for the Man in a Coat from *The Unknown Woman*, Moscow 1918   112
7 Dmitrievsky's lithograph, "On the Bridge", for Blok's play, *The Unknown Woman*, 1922   120

1. Aleksandr Blok in 1891–92
Courtesy of Union of Theater Workers' Library, Moscow

INTRODUCTION TO THE SERIES

The Russian Theatre Archive makes available in English the best avant-garde plays from the pre-Revolutionary period to the present day. It features monographs on major playwrights and theatre directors, introductions to previously unknown works, and studies of the main artistic groups and periods.

Plays are presented in performing edition translations, including (where appropriate) musical scores, and instructions for music and dance. Whenever possible the translated texts will be accompanied by videotapes of performances of plays in the original language.

2. Aleksandr Blok in 1911
Courtesy of Union of Theater Workers' Library, Moscow

INTRODUCTION
Exit from lyric isolation

I From lyric to drama

The dramas before you mark a break with the past. In them, Aleksandr Blok reappropriated his own work. As strange as it may sound, at the time he started writing these plays, Blok found his own image increasingly alien. Although the reading public had hailed his early poetry and recognized him as the best of the younger generation of Symbolists, this acclaim had come at a price: for the reading public refused to see him other than as the poet of a single, particular persona, the singer of the "Beautiful Lady." This persona, which grew quite naturally out of his first collection *Verses about the Beautiful Lady*, became a kind of cell Blok sought to escape from. The persona of his lyrics effectively set the bounds of the relation between his work and the world. After the 1905 Revolution, Blok felt stifled by these boundaries and began to seek a truer relation to the world. What he sought in the theater, he told the director Vsevolod Meyerhold, was "an exit from lyric isolation."[1]

The lyric isolation from which Blok sought an exit stemmed from a creative impasse. The poetry of Blok's first period is a poetry of mystic mood and incantation. Intimations of other worlds take precedence over this earth, over the here and now. Although Blok had already found his own voice, the influence of Russia's later Romantic poets, Afanasy Fet and Yakov Polonsky, is palpable. The defining influence on Blok's early poetry, however, is the poet and philosopher Vladimir Solovyov's cult of the World Soul, or the divine Sophia. Solovyov's Sophia was, for Blok, both revelation and enigma. On one hand, the early poetry is permeated by the poet's desire to reach Sophia, who mediates between God and man. On the other, her elusiveness engenders doubt.

Problems of a personal nature further complicated Blok's predicament:

---

1 Aleksandr Blok, *Sobranie sochinenii v vos'mi tomakh* (Moskva-Leningrad: Gosudarstvennoe izdatel'stvo khudozhestvennoi literatury, 1960–63), vol. 8: 170.

If at times Sophia assumed the characteristics of the Mother of God, at others she bore a striking resemblance to Blok's fiancée and later wife, Lyubov Mendeleeva.[2] The consequent confusion over his muse wreaked havoc not only on Blok and Mendeleeva's marriage, but also on his friendship with Andrei Bely, who went further than Blok by equating Mendeleeva and Sophia. The fact that both Blok and Bely felt their friendship to be mystically ordained because their first letters to one another had crossed in the mail could not disguise the growing tension in their relationship. After a series of misunderstandings, Bely eventually challenged Blok to a duel; and although the duel never came to pass, their friendship dissolved into something more like enmity. At a slightly later date, Bely went so far as to ask Mendeleeva to run off with him. She refused. Her marriage, however, would never be the same.

It was against the backdrop of the greater social upheaval of the 1905 Revolution and its aftermath that this personal drama unfolded. The revolution served as a wake-up call for Blok by challenging his notion of himself. If the persona of the *Verses about the Beautiful Lady* exists in a sphere abstracted from this world, the persona of Blok's second volume is a creature of this earth. In part, this growing preoccupation with this world grew out of experience. Blok was an eyewitness to the events of the 1905 Revolution. Whereas many of his class remained behind locked doors, Blok (and his mother) went outside. He was also acutely aware of the role his stepfather, a lieutenant in the Grenadier Guards, played in suppressing the revolt. The net effect of this experience was to highlight what was, for Blok anyway, a seemingly unbridgeable chasm between the intelligentsia and the people. This theme, which Blok would later call his own, would preoccupy the poet until the end of his life.

Such concerns about his place in the world reoriented Blok's reading and then his writing. At about this time, Blok fell under the spell of the work of an older Symbolist poet, Valery Bryusov. The latter's collection *Urbi et Orbi* renewed the language of Symbolism by introducing urban and naturalistic themes into the otherwise ethereal *topos* of Symbolist cosmology. For Blok, Bryusov's collection was suggestive. Although Blok did not simply dismiss mysticism as Bryusov did, he more and more clearly understood the limits of its role in this world and in his life. No longer content with a poetry of mystic revelation, he sought out other poets who concerned themselves with this world. Eventually, this search would lead him back to Nikolai Nekrasov and the tradition of civic realist verse in Russian. Nekrasov's influence is most pronounced in Blok's fourth drama, *The Song of Fate*, yet his example was already on

---

2 Mendeeleva was the daughter of the renowned chemist Dmitry Mendeleev, who formulated the periodic table.

Blok's mind. As Blok incorporated and internalized these influences, his poetry changed. The church is replaced by the tavern; the lofty-minded poet gives in to dissolution; and the Beautiful Lady finds herself out on the streets.

As striking as the transformation in Blok's poetry was, it does not, by itself, explain the image of the Beautiful Lady in the trilogy of lyric dramas. In composing them, Blok turned again to the example of Vladimir Solovyov. Apart from his philosophical works and poetry, Solovyov had also written a number of "joke dramas" [shutochnye dramy], or comic dramas. At Solovyov's time, such plays belonged to a decidedly minor, though productive genre. Perhaps the most famous examples of the genre issued from the fictive pen of the fictitious Kozma Prutkov. The brainchild of two poet-playwrights Aleksei Tolstoy and Aleksei Zhemchuzhnikov (who had a little help from the latter's brothers Vladimir and Aleksandr), Prutkov delivered a mixture of satire and parody in his plays, and the genre caught on. It, of course, never rivaled mainstream genres, such as tragedy, and Prutkov never threatened to supersede Ostrovsky. On the other hand, the genre's emphasis on parody gave a new lease on life to worn-out clichés and formulas. In Solovyov's case, parody gave way to self-parody as he sought to revitalize his own language. In the play *The White Lily*, for example, Solovyov poked fun at his own ideas about the divine Sophia. The search for the elusive feminine spirit leads the hero to a bear den. Although the hero's search is capped by a successful union with the spirit of the white lily, the idea of the divine Sophia is not treated solemnly. Solovyov intersplices farcical and serious elements throughout the play. Solovyov's example proved pivotal for Blok.[3]

What Blok found in *The White Lily* was the means to redefine his poetic idiom without renouncing his belief system. The Beautiful Lady remains, but dons a new mask. The poetic voice of the first collection also remains, but now it speaks with different intonations and in a different context. Moreover, other voices join in to challenge its authority. The seamless, monologic fabric of the lyrics is ripped apart by contending voices. Yet paradoxically, Blok's own voice is not diminished, but enhanced. His singularity shone through. In the end, Blok's reappropriation of his own past helped to distinguish him from his fellow Symbolists and to elaborate his poetic personality more fully. As he wrote to Bely at the time, "In the face of present conditions when everything is confused everywhere, my biggest wish is to be myself."[4] Self-knowledge came dearly: Friends turned into enemies, allies turned their backs. Yet, Blok did not relent. In the face of

---

3 For a more detailed discussion of this topic, see my article "The Ongoing Influence of V.S. Solov'ev on A.A. Blok," *Slavic and East European Journal*, 36, No. 4 (1992): 435–51.
4 Aleksandr Blok, *Sobranie sochinenii*, 8: 167.

Bely's sometimes bitter remonstrances, Blok still insisted, "I prefer to follow the precept – *remain who you yourself are.*"[5]

II The Commedia dell'Arte and the appropriation of the past: *A Puppet Show*

What endows these plays, and especially *A Puppet Show*, with such great cultural resonance is that Blok's individual need to reappropriate his own past coincided with a more general trend in Russian culture of the time to reconsider the past, a trend that is sometimes associated with what has come to be called a "reevaluation of all values" [pereotsenka vsekh tsennostei]. As the tenets of the immediate past – the tenets of realism and naturalism – were brought into question, poets, fiction writers, directors, composers, and visual artists cast back into the more distant past for "new" artistic models. Nowhere was this trend more strongly felt than in the theater. Nearly every major director after Stanislavsky and Nemirovich-Danchenko looked to the past for inspiration. In this sense, Nikolai Evreinov's Starinnyi, or Antiquarian Theater provides a kind of paradigm for the age: Evreinov and his colleagues proposed stagings in the manner of the major theatrical traditions of the past. In successive seasons, the company was to present plays of the Spanish Golden Age, scenarios of the *commedia dell'arte*, mystery plays of the medieval theater, and so on.[6] The enterprise failed when the Starinnyi folded, but its spirit was consonant with the age.

As he cast back into theatrical history, Blok discovered something new in the tradition of the *commedia dell'arte*, the beginnings of which date back to the first half of the sixteenth century.[7] How Blok decided on the *commedia dell'arte* remains open to question. On one hand, images and types from the *commedia* had entered Blok's creative world already by 1902, as is made clear by such poems as "Light staggered in the window" and "He showed up at a well-ordered ball." Moreover, Blok had worked out some aspects of *A Puppet Show* in lyric form in such poems as "At round tables, everybody was screaming," "At that hour when narcissuses are getting drunk," "You will dress me in silver," and "A Travelling Show" before he actually wrote the play itself. (All of these poems are to be found below in the section entitled "Context of *A Puppet Show*".) At about the same time, pictorial artists were turning to the *commedia* for inspiration, and they may have influenced Blok. For example, some years

---

5 Aleksandr Blok, *Sobranie sochinenii*, 8: 189.
6 It is perhaps worth noting that the Starinnyi staged Blok's translation of the trouvère poet Rutebuef's *Le Miracle de Théophile*.
7 As the names Pierrot, Columbine, and Harlequin make clear, Blok employed in *A Puppet Show* the *commedia dell'arte* in its later, French incarnation.

earlier, the artists associated with Sergei Diaghilev's journal *The World of Art* had introduced the figures of the *commedia dell'arte* into their paintings. Diaghilev himself contributed to the growing interest in the *commedia dell'arte* by including and highlighting in his journal and exhibitions artists from the past, such as Jean Watteau, and contemporary artists, such as Aubrey Beardsley, who drew on its tradition. Yet, Blok said nothing about any of these artists when he discussed *A Puppet Show*. None of the extant letters, notebooks, diaries, or even the memoirs of his contemporaries tells us anything about the influence of these artists on Blok. In all likelihood, their influence was limited since the genesis of the play suggests that the impetus to write *A Puppet Show* arose out of the theatrical tradition of the *commedia dell'arte*, and not its pictorial legacy.

At first, Blok did not conceive *A Puppet Show* in terms of the *commedia dell'arte*, or even as a play for that matter. In its first incarnation, *A Puppet Show* was a poem, utterly bereft of its later *commedia dell'arte* trappings. For its imagery, the poem (also included in this volume), relies on the tradition of Russian puppet theater, which exercised an enormous influence on Blok.[8] The *commedia dell'arte*, in contrast, does not inform the poem. The transition from poem to play, then, takes on added importance. Moreover, given the rather unique circumstances of that transition, this episode warrants further scrutiny.

Blok, as it turns out, wrote *A Puppet Show* on a commission of sorts. For some time, he had been frequenting the literary salon of his fellow Symbolist, Viacheslav Ivanov. Ivanov and his wife, the writer Lydia Zinovieva-Hannibal, held their Wednesday night meetings in their own apartment, which because of its salience came to be known simply as the "tower." Wednesday nights at the tower attracted the cultural elite of St. Petersburg. Ivanov's fellow Symbolists, of course, formed the core. Yet, they were joined by a heterogeneous group of people not necessarily associated with the Symbolists. Sympathetic poets, like Mikhail Kuzmin and Maximilian Voloshin, might mingle with professors from the University of St. Petersburg, such as the eminent classicist Faddei Zelinsky. Or the future Commissar of Education, Anatoly Lunacharsky, might bump into Akhmatova or Mandelshtam.[9] Theater people rounded out the crowd. Of the latter, it was Vsevolod Meyerhold who would play a key role in Blok's development as a dramatist.

A group, which included Blok, Meyerhold, Ivanov, and Georgy Chulkov, formed and met at Ivanov and Zinovieva-Hannibal's tower.

---

8 For more on this question, see Zinaida Mints, "V smyslovom prostrantsve *Balaganchika*," *Uchenye zapiski Tartuskogo Universiteta*, 720 (1986): 44–53.
9 For more on Ivanov's tower, see Avril Pyman, *The Life of Aleksandr Blok, Volume I: The Distant Thunder 1880–1908* (Oxford: Oxford University Press, 1979), vol. 1: 228ff.

Their dual aim consisted of publishing a literary miscellany and creating a theater, both to be called "The Torches." Of the two, only the miscellany saw light of day. However, before the demise of the theater project, the group had inveigled a very reluctant Blok to transform his poem "A Puppet Show" into a play. His reluctance notwithstanding, Blok worked quickly and finished the play in less than a month. A certain mystery lingers around the creation of *A Puppet Show*, as Blok maintained his habitual and customary magisterial silence about his working habits and about the work itself. The drafts afford us some small glimpse into Blok's creative process. The first draft makes no reference to the figures of the *commedia dell'arte*, which appear only later. Indeed, Blok seems, in the beginning, to have undertaken to write just such a play as the character of the Author claims to have written: that is, a love story about the "mutual love of two youthful souls," whose way is barred by a third person. Unlike his hapless Author, Blok grew dissatisfied with the result. At a later stage – although how exactly he came to this resolution remains unclear – he introduced the figures of the *commedia dell'arte* and thereby enriched the discourse of the play. Not only did Blok renew his own poetic idiom, he charted a new course for the drama of his time by reviving the theatrical language of the *commedia dell'arte*.

The immediate prospects for staging the play appeared dim with the failure of the theater "The Torches." Nonetheless, Meyerhold was enchanted with Blok's play and continued to look for an opportunity to stage it. When the great actress Vera Komissarzhevskaya reorganized her theater, she invited Meyerhold to assume the duties of company director. The Komissarzhevskaya Theater, or the Theater on Ofitserskaya Street as it came to be known, was in disarray when Meyerhold took over. The theater had arisen largely as a vehicle for Kommissarzhevskaya, whose popularity and acclaim as an actress were sufficient to get the enterprise off the ground. They were not enough, as it turned out, to sustain the theater.

However, the problem lay not in Komissarzhevskaya's decline as an actress or as a star with great drawing power, even if some scurrilous critics delighted in announcing her downfall, but rather in a fundamental shift in the organization of the Russian theater. The old system, in which the production was tailored to fit "star" actors and actresses and which had predominated through the end of the nineteenth century, came increasingly under fire because, more often than not, histrionics replaced acting, and artifice effaced art. Dissatisfaction with the old system first expressed itself in the form of amateur theatrical "circles," which began to levy a significant influence on theatrical life. Some of these circles generated sufficient momentum to develop into independent theaters. The most famous example is the Moscow Art Theater, where Meyerhold got his start as an actor. The Moscow Theater is not only an exemplary theater of its time, but also a representative one, in which the theatrical tendencies that characterize the Russian theater of the turn of the century can be seen with great clarity. Stanislavsky and Nemirovich-Danchenko subordinated actor to ensemble, a principle that led to the concomitant strengthening of the director. The theater of the star gave way to the theater of the director. Decisions about repertoire, staging, costuming, casting – in other words, all the salient decisions of the theater's creative life – fell to the director. More and more through the two decades preceding the Revolution, theaters were organized around directors, not actors.

It is to Komissarzhevskaya's credit that she sensed the approaching change. In no small part, she started her own company in order to introduce new, contemporary plays into the repertoire. On the other hand, she was still a product of the old system and never completely reconciled herself to the idea of a director's theater. She found herself increasingly out of place in her own theater. Inevitably, her collaboration with Meyerhold was to be short-lived, lasting barely fifteen months. Yet, in that short time, a revolution in theater took place. The beginnings of that revolution were conventional enough: a triumphant, if tried and true staging of *Hedda Gabler* that showed off to great effect Komissarzhevskaya's talent. From there, Meyerhold elaborated a new language of Symbolist theater in stagings of Mæterlinck's *Sister Beatrice* [*La soeur Béatrice*] and Przybyszewski's *Eternal Fairytale* [*Odwieczna baśń*]. However, these productions were merely innovative. The revolution itself came on December 30, 1906, with the première of *A Puppet Show*.

As a renowned scholar and historian of the Russian stage put it, "Blok's *A Puppet Show* was one of the central events in the history of the Russian theater at the beginning of the century."[10] It was also one of the most controversial, superseded only perhaps by the première of Stravinsky's *Rite of Spring* some years later. When the curtain fell on *A Puppet Show*, part of the audience broke into thunderous applause, while the other hissed, whistled, and hollered at the top of its collective lungs. In their memoirs, a number of those present recall ecstatic exclamations of approbation mixing with questions born of sheer consternation and with angry vituperations against the poet and the director. The reviews, with a few important exceptions, were negative. One critic, still bristling days later, insisted that the play made fun of the public, while another dismissed it as unworthy of people of common sense. Negative appraisals, such as these, were not uncommon, even later. However, other commentators, perhaps more thoughtful and certainly less judgmental, understood that theatrical discourse had changed irrevocably.

---

10 Konstantin Rudnitskii, "Rezhisserskoe iskusstvo." In Dmitriev, Iurii, Tat'iana Rodina, Oleg Fel'dman, Efim Kholodov, and Tat'iana Shakh-Azizova (eds.), *Istoriia russkogo dramaticheskogo teatra v semi tomakh* (Moskva: Iskusstvo, 1987), vol. 7: 140.

What Blok and Meyerhold created in *A Puppet Show* was theatrical discourse of startling and profound complexity and originality. The negative satire that many of the first critics attributed to the play, in fact, proved to be something far more productive and positive. The masks and the antics of the *commedia dell'arte* resuscitate the moribund traditions of the theater of the actor, the high Symbolist theater, and Greek choral tragedy. For example, the play opens with the so-called "mystic" scene, which is reminiscent of Mæterlinck's drama. With the appearance of Pierrot, however, the serious import of such a high Symbolist scene is undermined and thrown into question. The doubts he raises about the mystics' conception of Columbine as Death reveal the limitations of their world view and its meaning. Likewise, Harlequin's appearance later in the play as a coryphaeus at the head of a chorus undermines the usually serious import of the choral song. In both cases, satire is involved, but it does not exhaust the meaning of these scenes. Rather, the juxtaposition of these different theatrical traditions, far from negating their respective meanings, transforms them and creates new meaning through what the Russian philosopher Mikhail Bakhtin has called "mésalliances."[11] In this sense, Blok's appropriation of the past turns out to be profoundly productive and positive.

Blok's use of the *commedia dell'arte* also informs the immanent discourse of the play. In this regard, the mode of Pierrot's appearance on stage takes on particular importance. His clothing consists of a theatrical costume, which not only clashes with the mystics' frock coats, but indeed reveals a hidden truth about them: Their apparent verisimilitude notwithstanding, the frock coats are also theatrical costumes. By his very appearance, Pierrot draws the audience's attention to the play's artifice and to its multi-layered discourse. The moment the curtain rises, not only do two theatrical traditions clash, but so do two modes of artistic representation: theater as verisimilitude and theater as artifice. Blok creates in *A Puppet Show* a theatrical metalanguage, that is, a discourse by means of which the play comments on itself, and he continues to develop it consistently throughout the play. The Author, for instance, sounds this theme again when he rushes out on stage to complain about the play. Not only is this an effective example of comic relief, but it raises again the question of what the real nature of the play is. Although the Author insists that he wrote "a most realistic play," the events that have already transpired on stage contradict him and suggest that the play is about something else entirely. The meaning of the play again proves problematic when Harlequin makes his exit: Harlequin "jumps through the window. The

---

11 See, for instance, Mikhail Bakhtin, *Problems of Dostoevsky's Poetics* (Minneapolis: University of Minnesota Press, 1984), 123.

distance, visible through the window, turns out to be painted on paper. The paper rips. Harlequin flies head over heels into the void." Here, Blok toys again with the meaning of the play, which proves to be both reality and illusion at the same moment. The play's finale serves as a kind of coda: Just as the Author is about to unite his star-crossed hero and heroine, the scenery flies up, and the artifice of the play is yet again laid bare. As soon as he comprehends the meaning of his predicament, the Author runs off, leaving Pierrot alone on stage. The illusion of theater is underscored; yet, the pathos of Pierrot's position remains. Perhaps nowhere is this ambivalence so pronounced as in the image of Columbine, who is alternately incarnated as Pierrot's bride-to-be, Death itself, and a cardboard cutout.

Meyerhold's production served to transpose Blok's innovations onto the stage. Together with the stage designer Nikolai Sapunov, Meyerhold created sets that drew attention to the play's artifice and, thus, to the theater as theater.[12] In the first scene, for example, Meyerhold arranged a "long table, covered to the floor with black cloth, parallel to the footlights. Behind the table sit 'mystics' in such a way that the audience sees only the upper part of their figures. Having become frightened at a particular cue, the mystics lower their heads in such a way that suddenly behind the table there remain only busts without heads and without arms. It turns out that it was *from cardboard* that the contours of the figures had been cut, and frock coats, shirtfronts, collars and cuffs had been drawn on them with charcoal and chalk. The actors' arms had been thrust through round openings cut into the cardboard busts, and their heads had only rested against the cardboard collars."[13] The usual theatrical conceit of actor-as-character is here compounded by the further artifice of character-as-cutout. The audience is forced to recognize the theatricality of this scene. Meyerhold went further in laying bare his artifice in the construction of a theater within the theater, a puppet show within a puppet show: "The 'theatrolet' [*teatrik*] has its own stage, its own curtain, its own prompt box, its own portals and wings. The upper part of the 'theatrolet' is not covered by the traditional 'harlequin.' The gridiron with all its ropes and wires is in full view of the public. When the set flies up in the little 'theatrolet' into the real gridiron of the theater, the audience can see all of its movements."[14] With every new invention, Meyerhold drew the audience's attention back to what they were actually watching, namely a piece for theater, and away from what they seemed to be watching, that is, the play.

---

12 Music for the play was written by the poet and composer Mikhail Kuzmin.
13 Meierkhol'd, Vsevolod, "Balagan." In his *Stat'i, pis'ma, rechi, besedy, chast' pervaia 1891–1917* (Moskva: Iskusstvo, 1968), vol. 1: 228.
14 Meierkhol'd, Vsevolod, "Primechaniia k spisku rezhisserskikh rabot." In his *Stat'i, pis'ma, rechi, besedy, chast' pervaia 1891–1917* (Moskva: Iskusstvo, 1968), 1: 250.

In this sense, Meyerhold's approach is analogous to Blok's: The past becomes a means to generate new meaning. To no small degree, the consonance in their approaches explains the success of the production at the Komissarzhevskaya Theater.

III Of royalty and revolution: *The King on the Square*

To judge only by its prologue, *The King on the Square* would seem to be cut from the same cloth as *A Puppet Show*: A similar concern for theatrical metalanguage makes itself felt almost immediately. As soon as the Fool puts to shore, he launches into a monologue that, from the beginning, lays bare the artifice of the play:

> . . . I found my way
>   And sailed in here,
> So as to mollify you a little, ladies
>   And gentlemen, with my good sense.
>
> So here is a palace on the dark background,
>   And on the terrace – a throne.
> A King, as you see, wears his crown.
>   He is old, despondent.

Not only does the Fool set the scene for the audience, but he makes clear that what is to transpire before them is a play. If, in its beginnings, the prologue takes on the character of an introduction, its function becomes more radical, the further it progresses:

> Here is the way for the pure public.
>   Here's a bench that's for it.
> And I have sat down on it
>   Only by right of the Prologue.
>
> In front of me, the sea is in the orchestra.
>   Its waves are dark.
> But if the sun soon rises,
>   I'll see it to its depths.
>
> My duty was just to force you
>   To cast your glance on this view.

With these words, the Fool compels the audience to see the play as a play. By invoking the term "prologue," the Fool effectively prevents the audience from apprehending the play as a representation of reality. He casts doubt on its mimetic function and thereby underscores its artifice. The inherent implications of this invocation become explicit when he observes that "the sea is in the orchestra." In this sense, the Fool clowns with the conventions of theater and leads the audience to consider the nature of these conventions.

Yet, the prologue proves to be a bravura of misdirection, for Blok does not develop the implications of his theatrical metalanguage in *The King on the Square* as he did in *A Puppet Show*. Instead, he turns to deal in a more straightforward manner with the theme of politics and the politics of power in particular. *The King on the Square* does not represent Blok's first treatment of this theme. Not surprisingly, Blok's first pass at this theme was in lyric poetry. As a general rule, the early lyrics devoted to this theme are among Blok's very weakest, and this is especially true of the narrative poem *Her Coming*, which is closely tied to *The King on the Square* in terms of both its plot and its imagery. Blok considered *Her Coming* such a weak work that he excluded it from the third edition of his *Collected Poems* (1916), only to then restore it in the fourth edition. Blok's misgivings and rationale for including the poem are clear already in his notes to the second edition, where he wrote, "I have decided to place here this weak and unfinished poem because it is characteristic of the book and of that time as it is devoted to certain 'unrealized hopes' (according to my conception of it then).... Development of the same theme may be found in the lyric drama *The King on the Square*."[15] (For much the same reason, the reader will find a translation of *Her Coming* in the section entitled "Context of *The King on the Square*" below.) It is here that Blok, for the first time, broaches a theme he will pursue through lyric poems, essays, and epic poems until the end of his career: the intelligentsia and the people.

From this point of view, *Her Coming* and *The King on the Square* mark an important transition in Blok's work. If the result sometimes borders on allegory, such weaknesses should not obscure the complexity of what Blok assays. In the play, the forces at work in the society Blok portrays align themselves in stark contrasts: Hunger and want have ravaged the faith of the poor in the King who rules them. Revolutionaries attempt to exploit the growing unrest to overthrow the government. In opposition to them stands the Architect who, as we discover at the end of the play, sculpted the stone King with his own hands. The Architect insists on the status quo. His own Daughter, however, opposes him. She heralds idealistic change, not revolution, but a rejuvenation of the current system. By sacrificing her body to the King, she believes, she will resuscitate his

---

15 Cited according to Vladimir Orlov, "Primechaniia," in Aleksandr Blok, *Sobranie sochinenii* 2: 392.

moribund form. Counterposed to the dream of the Architect's Daughter, the Fool trumpets common sense. He attempts to ensnare the Poet, who is caught in the middle, unable to decide which is the right path.

The Poet's dilemma assumed particular importance for Blok and led to a bifurcation in his work on *The King on the Square*. The arguments for civic poetry that receive brief treatment in the play come in for closer scrutiny in Blok's dramatic dialogue *Of Love, Poetry, and Government Service* (also included in the section entitled "Context of *The King on the Square*" below). In the dialogue, Blok looks back to the example of Pushkin's "The Bookseller's Conversation with the Poet," which also deals with the poet's relation to society. Pushkin examines what was at the time a new role for the poet in society. In Pushkin's generation the possibility of writing as a profession was becoming a reality, and Pushkin delved into the impact that this change would have on writers. Blok transposes Pushkin's concerns about commercial relations to the realm of political relations.

When Blok turned to the play, however, his concern for political relations was reified not in Pushkin's terms, but in Dostoevsky's. At the end of the play after the final cataclysm, the Architect delivers his final monologue. Not only the general themes, but often the very phrases he chooses echo the Grand Inquisitor sequence in *The Brothers Karamazov*. Just as the Grand Inquisitor insists that men harbor a craven fear of freedom and secretly wish to be ruled, so too the Architect tells the people that he has given them what they desired: the King, an image of power. Just as the Grand Inquisitor tells his silent interlocutor that whoever controls the supply of bread controls the people, so too the Architect couches his remarks about human happiness in terms of bread. The parallels are strident and suggest that the Architect, like the Grand Inquisitor before him, would engineer human souls.

It was perhaps Blok's candor in his treatment of matters politic that eventually led to an impasse with the censor. The play was rejected as unfit for public performance, though it did make its way into print. Meyerhold took an avid interest in the play and maintained that interest long after the initial rejection by the censor. As late as 1923, Meyerhold announced plans to stage *The King on the Square* in an all Blok program, which was to also include Blok's last play *Ramses* and a dramatization of his epic poem *The Twelve*. The program was never realized, but it does attest to the enduring value the play retained for Meyerhold.

On the other hand, the play's weaknesses are significant. For instance, given the relatively limited scope of the play, a certain disproportion becomes apparent: The main characters do not make their appearance until the second act. As a result, the play's dramatic tension goes somewhat slack, and the main characters never receive adequate development. That Blok observes the classical unities of time and place does not reverse this tendency. Yet, the lessons learned in the writing of *The King on the Square* are not lost on Blok, and his next play too would profit from his ongoing reappropriation of Dostoevsky.

IV "To be" incarnate: *The Unknown Woman*

The Unknown Woman, not unlike *A Puppet Show*, grew directly out of a poem bearing the same title. The genesis of the play remains somewhat obscure because Blok referred to it in only the most cursory way as he worked on it. What is clear, however, is the relation between the play and various poems Blok wrote at about the same time. Numerous motifs and images make their first appearance in such poems as "The Unknown Woman," "There, in the hard, howling frost of the night," "Star-strewn train," "Your face is paler than it was," and "There ladies flaunt fashions," only to be transformed in the play. (See the section entitled "Context of *The Unknown Woman*" below.) In the play, these themes and motifs are developed in a different direction, largely owing to the influence of Dostoevsky, which becomes immediately apparent.

To the title page of *The Unknown Woman* Blok appends two epigraphs from Dostoevsky's *The Idiot*, and they seem to serve straightforward purposes. The first introduces the theme of an elusive beauty, and the second presents a recognition scene about two people who believe they have met before. Both themes are central to *The Unknown Woman*, and the significance of the epigraphs appears restricted. Closer examination, however, reveals that *The Idiot* informs *The Unknown Woman* in other, important ways. The problem of the love triangle, so central to Dostoevsky's novel, plays no less a role in Blok's play. Construed more largely, this influence grows out of Dostoevsky's poetics and not only *The Idiot*. For example, the double, a pivotal figure in much of Dostoevsky's fiction, also haunts Blok's play.

Blok develops the double beyond the realm of character and introduces it in unexpected areas. The structure of the play turns out to be composed, in fact, of a series of parallelisms. Not only do characters double each other, but entire scenes and acts double one another. The first and third "visions," as Blok calls the acts of the play, resemble each other down to minute details. The high society drawing room of the third vision turns out to be an uncanny replica of the bar that serves as the setting of the first vision. The aristocrats who debate Serpantini's risqué dance in the third vision echo the drunks who argue with the Seminarian about a dancing girl in the first. The visions replay scenes and conversations so accurately that even specific phrases are repeated. Yet, this parallelism serves as mere background, against which difference becomes apparent. And the greatest difference between the first and third visions arises towards the end of each, with the appearance of a female figure.

In the first vision, the female figure, or more accurately figurine, is a cameo that a patron of the bar sells to the Poet. In the third, the Unknown Woman, or Maria as she likes to be called, enters the drawing room. The difference is striking. It serves to mark what is key to the play: the reappropriation of the Beautiful Lady. Late in the third vision, the Hostess imposes on the Poet, asking him to grace the company gathered there with a reading of his verse. She announces to her guests, "Our beautiful poet will read for us a beautiful poem again about, I hope, the beautiful lady." The Poet complies and begins to recite a poem about the Beautiful Lady, which is interrupted by the entrance of the Unknown Woman. It so resembles Blok's early work that it could be taken from *Verses about the Beautiful Lady*. Yet, Blok's reappropriation of his earlier manner diverges radically from the Poet's intent. The difference between Blok's discourse and the Poet's reveals an irony that is characteristic of Blok's second period.

This irony finds expression in various elements of the play and marks a return to the concern for theatrical metalanguage that first appeared in *A Puppet Show*. At key junctures, the play forces the reader or spectator to recognize its theatricality. In the second vision, for example, a star falls to earth and becomes incarnated as a woman. The conventions of the realist stage are abandoned altogether. Even the stage directions compel reader and spectator to reconsider basic assumptions about the theater. The stage directions do not demarcate the boundaries between acts as they usually do in realist plays. Instead, they function as segues that underscore the continuity of the action. The transition from the first vision to the second will serve to illustrate this point:

The whole bar seems to have dived somewhere. The walls part. The ceiling, having tilted once and for all, opens up the sky – wintry, blue, cold. In the deep blue evening snows opens:

THE SECOND VISION

The same evening. The end of a street at the edge of the city. The last houses, breaking off suddenly, reveal a wide perspective: A dark, empty bridge across a big river. Quiet boats with signal lights slumber along both sides of the bridge. An avenue, endless, straight as an arrow, and framed by rows of streetlights and trees that are white from hoarfrost, stretches beyond the bridge. In the air, the snow flutters down and turns starry.

The flow of one scene into another reveals unexpected similarities between the two, and assumptions in realist theater about absolutely discrete and independent settings fall by the wayside. In new and innovative ways, Blok pushes the metalanguage of theater into new domains.

When Meyerhold staged *The Unknown Woman* in 1914,[16] it was precisely these elements that he brought out. Theatricality became an end in itself. As one commentator observes, "There was one moment which made theatrical history, when the grey figures knelt down with lighted candles forming a line of living footlights reminiscent of the theatre of the eighteenth century."[17] Meyerhold himself saw the production as the beginning of a new movement in theater: "The erection of the bridge for the second part of Blok's *The Unknown Woman* in Petrograd in 1914 (the collaborative work of Vsevolod Meyerhold and Iurii M. Bondi) on the platform of the 'Tenishevsky auditorium,' which was free from theatrical elements, was the first attempt at the mounting of a stage area under the badge of constructivism."[18] Meyerhold pursued a conception of theater as theater and introduced elements of various theatrical traditions. The entire performance, which consisted of a twin bill that included both *The Unknown Woman* and *A Puppet Show*, spanned theatrical traditions as disparate as the *commedia dell'arte* and the eighteenth-century theater. Perhaps the most startling incorporation of a theatrical tradition came during the interlude: "After *The Unknown Woman* was finished, onto the stage came juggling Chinese children, who in the capacity of the interlude, did a series of simple tricks, and the participants in the plays tossed real oranges out to the audience."[19] The mode and the matter were well suited to one another. Blok's reappropriation of the poetry of the Beautiful Lady found its reflection in Meyerhold's reappropriation of the theater of the past.[20]

V Exit from lyric isolation

When writing about *A Puppet Show*, *The King on the Square*, and *The Unknown Woman* as a group of plays, commentators bandy about the term "trilogy," which raises the very real question of what these plays have in common. Does the term trilogy apply to them at all? Certainly, not in the conventional sense. That is, they do not represent successive events, such as we find in Aleksei Tolstoy's trilogy of historical dramas *The Death of Ivan the Terrible*, *Tsar Fyodor*, and *Tsar Boris*. Nor do characters from

---

16 The censor blocked production of *The Unknown Woman* early on, and nearly eight years were to pass before Meyerhold was able to realize his long-standing dream to stage it.
17 Avril Pyman, *The Life of Aleksandr Blok*, 2: 200.
18 Vsevolod Meierkhol'd, *Stat'i, pis'ma, rechi, besedy*, 2: 18.
19 Nikolai Volkov, *Meierkhol'd*, 2 v. (Moskva-Leningrad: Academia, 1929), 2: 321.
20 On the other hand, not everyone present was aware of the significance of the performance. The reviews were largely negative. Even Blok had doubts about the first performance. However, when he returned several nights later, the production enchanted him, and he regretted missing the intervening performances.

one play appear in the other plays, as happens in Aleksandr Sukhovo-Kobylin's dramatic trilogy *Krechinsky's Wedding*, *The Case*, and *Tarelkin's Death*. Yet, for all their variety, these plays display a unity that is real, but not readily apparent.

In all three plays, the main characters form a love triangle which derives from the *commedia dell'arte*. The triangle consists of a woman who is desired; a dreamy, but ineffectual suitor; and an aggressive and authoritative figure who exerts inexplicable control over the woman. As we move from one play to the next, Harlequin desires Columbine, the Poet longs for the Architect's Daughter, and another and different Poet in *The Unknown Woman* yearns for a star named Maria. Directly through their personal intervention or indirectly through the intervention of their work, Harlequin, the Architect, and the Astronomer effectively prevent these couples from uniting. In *A Puppet Show*, Harlequin has only to snap his fingers, and Columbine abandons Pierrot to follow him. In *The King on the Square*, it is the collapse of the Architect's creation, the King, that destroys both the Poet and the Architect's Daughter just at that moment when the Poet believes they will be united. Nor is the situation fundamentally different in *The Unknown Woman*, where the Astronomer's steps cut off the Poet as the latter approaches Maria. In the first two plays, the triangle is complicated by a buffoonish character (the Author in *A Puppet Show* and the Fool in *The King on the Square*), who claims to have some control over the proceedings. At times doubles complicate these relations and motifs may be attenuated in one play as compared with another, but still these basic relations obtain throughout.

These relations, especially where the lead female character is concerned, are characterized by a tendency toward the inanimate, towards rigidification. Columbine, the Architect's Daughter, and the Unknown Woman either become actually inanimate in the course of the action, or they sacrifice themselves to an inanimate object. In *A Puppet Show* and *The Unknown Woman*, we encounter the former: Columbine, under Harlequin's influence, falls prostrate on the ground and turns to cardboard; while the Unknown Woman, at the entrance of the Astronomer, reverts to a shining star. The case of the Architect's Daughter is somewhat attenuated, by comparison: She sacrifices her body to the inanimate stone statue of the King, sculpted by her father, the Architect. As the evidence of memoirs and Blok's own notebooks makes clear, it is Pushkin's influence that is to be felt here. Distant echoes from *The Bronze Horseman*, *The Golden Cockerel*, and *The Stone Guest* are to be heard in Blok's first three plays. Blok's treatment of this theme differs from Pushkin's, but the lineage is apparent.

The plays also share a common preoccupation with dramatic and theatrical metalanguage. Whether in the Author in *A Puppet Show* who elucidates the play's meaning for the benefit of the audience, or in the Fool in *The King on the Square* who reveals the play's artifice to the spectators, or in the stridently anti-realistic stage directions in *The Unknown Woman*, Blok consistently and carefully develops metadrama; that is, drama that explicitly acknowledges its dramatic nature and comments on it. If the affinity of Blok's trilogy of lyric dramas to the work of later dramatists like Pirandello is unmistakable, it should not obscure Blok's debt to the past, whether to the *commedia dell'arte* or the legacy of romantic drama. Blok's interest in metadrama reflects yet another dimension of his reappropriation of the past. By creating discourse in which traditions of the past are made to comment on one another, Blok revivified them, made them new. Just as his appropriation of his own past revitalized his poetic language, so his appropriation of theatrical traditions of the past revitalized drama. In this regard, his first three dramas are part of a single, common dramatic enterprise and should thus be viewed as a trilogy.

This common dramatic enterprise ceased to be a theatrical enterprise with the 1914 production of *A Puppet Show* and *The Unknown Woman*, when Blok's collaboration with Meyerhold broke off. The ins and outs of their relationship exceed the scope of this introduction, but it should be noted that Blok's path as a dramatist headed in a very different direction after the trilogy of lyric dramas. He pledged his next two plays, *The Song of Fate* and *The Rose and the Cross*, to Stanislavsky and the Moscow Art Theater. His growing predilection for what he called "healthy realism" led Blok to put greater and greater emphasis on the psychological and motivational development of the dramatic material. Yet despite this later divergence from the poetics of *A Puppet Show*, *The King on the Square*, *The Unknown Woman*, Blok's reputation as a dramatist rests almost entirely on his collaboration with Meyerhold. In their mutual preoccupation with the traditions of the past, they worked out a stage language which is fundamental to the modernist conception of theater. Although neglected throughout the Soviet era, these plays helped to define the modern and the modernist theater. In them, old traditions found new life, and a new theater found its voice.

A PUPPET SHOW

Dedicated
to
Vsevolod Emilievich Meyerhold

Dramatis Personae

COLUMBINE
PIERROT
HARLEQUIN
MYSTICS of both sexes in frock coats and fashionable gowns,
 and then in masks and masquerade costumes
CHAIRMAN of a mystical gathering
Three Pairs of Lovers
CLOWN
AUTHOR

An ordinary theater room with three walls, a window, and a door. Mystics of both sexes in frock coats and fashionable gowns sit at an illuminated table with a concentrated look on their faces. At a little distance, by the window, sits Pierrot in white overalls, pensive, downcast, pale, without mustache or eyebrows, like all Pierrots.

The Mystics are silent for some time.

> FIRST MYSTIC.   Do you hear?
> SECOND MYSTIC.   Yes.
> THIRD.   The event transpires.
> PIERROT. O, eternal horror, eternal gloom.
> FIRST MYSTIC. Do you wait?
> SECOND MYSTIC.   I wait.
> THIRD MYSTIC.   Near is the arrival.
>   Beyond the window, the wind gave us an omen.
> PIERROT. Unfaithful one, where are you? A long chain
>   Of street lamps stretches through the sleepy streets,
>   And the lovers go, pair by pair,
>   Warmed by their love's light.
>   Where are you? Why can't we, after the last pair,
>   Step into the circle meant for us?
>   I will go and strum my sad guitar
>   Under the window, where you dance in your friends' chorus!
>   I will rouge my face, so pale and moon-like,
>   Draw my brows and glue a mustache on.
>   Do you hear my poor heart, Columbine,
>   Draw out, draw out its melancholy song?

(Pierrot falls into a reverie and then livens up. But the anxious Author scrambles out from behind the curtain at the side.)

> AUTHOR. What's he saying? Esteemed members of the audience! I hurry to assure you that this actor is cruelly making fun of my authorial rights. The action takes place in Petersburg in wintertime. Just where did he get the window and guitar? I wrote my drama, not for a puppet theater ... I assure you ...

(Having suddenly become embarrassed by his own unexpected appearance, he hides behind the curtain again.)

PIERROT.

(*He has paid no attention to the Author. He is sitting, and he sighs pensively.*)

    Columbine!
FIRST MYSTIC.   You hear?
SECOND MYSTIC.   Yes.
THIRD MYSTIC. The maiden draws near from a distant country.
FIRST MYSTIC. O, like marble – her features.
SECOND MYSTIC.   O, in her eyes – emptiness.
THIRD MYSTIC. O, what whiteness and what purity.
FIRST MYSTIC. She'll approach and immediately our voices will have died.
SECOND MYSTIC. Yes. The silence will come.
THIRD MYSTIC.   But for long?
FIRST MYSTIC.   O, yes.
SECOND MYSTIC. White, all white as the snows.
THIRD MYSTIC.   Over her shoulders, a braid.[21]
FIRST MYSTIC. Who is she?

(*The Second Mystic bends over and whispers something in the ear of the First.*)

SECOND MYSTIC.   You won't give me away?
FIRST MYSTIC. (*In unfeigned horror.*)
    No, never.

(*The Author frightenedly leans out again, but quickly disappears, as if someone had dragged him back by the tails of his jacket.*)

PIERROT. (*As before, pensively.*)
    Columbine! Come here!
FIRST MYSTIC.   Be quiet! Don't you hear her footfall?
SECOND MYSTIC. I can hear her rustling and sighs.
THIRD MYSTIC.   O, who is among us?
FIRST MYSTIC. Who's at the window?
SECOND MYSTIC.   And who's at the door?
THIRD MYSTIC.   Can't see anything at all.
FIRST MYSTIC. Light the way. At this hour isn't it she who has come?

---

21 Blok introduces at this juncture a vital, but untranslatable, motif for the first time. The word "kosa" means either "braid" or "scythe," and Blok exploits both meanings throughout this and other texts.

A Puppet Show

(*The Second Mystic raises a candle. Completely unexpectedly and who knows from where, an unusually beautiful woman with a simple and tranquil face of a dull whiteness appears by the table. She is in white. The gaze of her placid eyes is indifferent. Behind her shoulders lies a plaited braid.*

The woman stands motionless. An ecstatic Pierrot prayerfully kneels. Tears, one can clearly see, choke him. Everything for him is unutterable.

In horror the mystics lean back against the backs of their chairs. The leg of one of them dangles helplessly. Another makes strange movements with his hand. A third stares wide-eyed. Having come to after some time, they whisper loudly.

    – *She's arrived!*
    – *How white her clothes are!*
    – *The emptiness in her eyes!*
    – *Her features are pale as marble!*
    – *Behind her shoulder – a scythe.*
    – *This is Death!*

Pierrot has heard. Having arisen slowly, he approaches the girl, takes her by the hand and leads her to the middle of the stage. He speaks in a voice as sonorous and joyful as the first peal of a bell.)

   PIERROT. Ladies and gentlemen! You are making a mistake! This is Columbine! This is my bride!

(*General horror. They throw their hands up in horror. The tails of frock coats flap. The Chairman of the meeting solemnly approaches Pierrot.*)

   CHAIRMAN. You've gone out of your mind. All evening we have awaited certain events. Our waiting is at an end. She has come to us, – the tranquil deliverer. Death has visited us.
   PIERROT. (*In a sonorous, child-like voice.*) I'm not listening to any fairy tales. I'm a simple person. You won't fool me. This is Columbine. This is my bride.
   CHAIRMAN. Ladies and gentlemen! Our poor friend has gone out of his mind from fear. He never thought about what we have been preparing for our entire lives. He didn't plumb the depths and prepare to humbly meet the Pale Friend at the final hour. We magnanimously forgive the simpleton. (*Addresses Pierrot.*) Brother, you can remain here no more. You will interfere with our last supper. But, I ask you, look one more time into her features: Do you see how white her clothes are, and

what paleness in her features? Oh, she is as white as the snow-caps on the summits! Her orbs reflect a mirror-like emptiness. Do you really not see the scythe behind her shoulders? Do you not recognize Death?

PIERROT. (*Across his pale face wanders a perplexed smile.*) I'm leaving. Either you're right, and I'm an unfortunate madman, or you've gone out of your minds, and I'm alone, misunderstood, and lovelorn. Bear me, blizzard, along the streets! O, eternal horror! Eternal gloom!

COLUMBINE. (*Follows Pierrot as he leaves.*) I won't abandon you.

(*Pierrot stops, perplexed. The Chairman beseechingly folds his arms.*)

CHAIRMAN. Light phantom! We have waited our whole lives for you! Don't forsake us!

(*A well-built youth in a Harlequin costume appears. The bells on him sing in silvery voices.*)

HARLEQUIN. (*Walks up to Columbine.*)
I'm waiting for you at the crossroads, darling,
In the grayish twilight of a winter's day.
Over you my blizzard sings,
Jingling my bells for you.

(*He puts his hand on Pierrot's shoulder. Pierrot falls flat on his back and lies in his white overalls without movement. Harlequin leads Columbine away by the hand. She smiles at him. General despondency. Everyone hangs lifelessly on their chairs. The sleeves of their frock-coats have stretched and cover their hands, as if there were no hands. Their heads have gone into their collars. It appears that empty frock-coats hang on the chairs. Suddenly Pierrot jumps up and runs off. The curtains close. At the same moment the disheveled and agitated Author darts out on the stageboards in front of the curtain.*)

AUTHOR. Kind sirs and madams! I offer you my most profound apologies, but I deny any responsibility! They mock me. I wrote a most realistic play, the essence of which I consider it my duty to set forth before you in a few words: The gist of it concerns the mutual love of two youthful souls. A third person bars their way, the barriers fall away in the end, and the lovers are united forevermore in lawful wedlock! I never decked my heroes out in fool's costumes! Without my knowledge, they have been performing some antiquated legend! I don't

A Puppet Show

acknowledge any legends, myths, or any other such banality! And especially allegorical plays on words: It is indecent to call a woman's braid the scythe of Death! That defames the ladies' estate. Kind sirs . . .

(A hand thrust out from behind the curtain grabs the Author by the collar. He disappears with a scream into the wings. The curtains quickly draw apart. A ball. The maskers circle under the quiet strains of a dance. Amongst them walk other maskers, knights, ladies, clowns.

A melancholy Pierrot sits in the middle of the stage on the bench, where Venus and Tannhauser usually kiss.)

PIERROT.
>I stood between two streetlights
>And listened to their voices
>As they whispered, huddled in their coats.
>Night kissed them on the eyes.
>
>And the silver blizzard twined
>A wedding ring for them.
>And I saw right through the night – my girlfriend
>Smiled into his face.
>
>Oh, then he seated my girlfriend
>In a cabman's sleigh.
>In a frosty mist I wandered,
>Following them from far away.
>
>Oh, he entangled her in nets,
>And, laughing, jingled his bell!
>But when he wrapped her up,
>Face down, oh, my girlfriend fell!
>
>He didn't offend her in the least,
>But my girlfriend fell into the snow!
>She couldn't stay up in her seat! . . .
>I couldn't stay my laughter! . . .
>
>And under the dance of frosty needles,
>Around my cardboard girl,
>He jumped up high and jingled.
>After him around the sleigh, I whirled!

And we sang on a sleepy street:
"Oh, what misfortune has befallen us!"
Above my cardboard girl – overhead
A star shone green on high.

All night long, through snowy streets,
We wandered – Pierrot and Harlequin . . .
He pressed into me so tenderly –
He tickled my nose with a feather!

He whispered to me: "Together, my brother,
We're inseparable for many days . . .
I'll grieve with you about your bride,
About your cardboard fiancée!"

(Pierrot sadly withdraws. After some time a pair of lovers are revealed on the same bench. He is in blue, she is in pink, their masks are the color of their clothes. They imagine themselves in a church and look upward at the cupolas.)

SHE.
    Dear, you whisper – "Lean . . ."
    I look up at the cupola, my face upturned.
HE.
    I look up at extraordinary heights –
    There, where the cupola accepts the evening-glow.
SHE.
    How decrepit the gilt is overhead,
    How the icons overhead glimmer.
HE.
    Our sleepy story is so quiet.
    You closed your eyes without sin.

(A kiss.)

SHE.
    . . . Someone dark is standing by the column
    And winks his cunning pupil!
    I fear you, lover!
    Let me cover up with your cloak!

(Silence.)

HE.
>   Look how peaceful the candles are,
>   How dawn has broken in the cupolas.

SHE.
>   Yes. Our meetings are so sweet.
>   Though I gave myself to you.

(She nestles into him. The quiet dance of the maskers and clowns hides the first pair from the audience. A second pair of lovers bursts into the middle of the dance. In front – she is in a black mask and a swirling red cloak. Behind – he, all in black, is lithe in his red mask and black cloak. His movements are impetuous. He chases after her, now overtaking her, now outstripping her. A whirlwind of cloaks.)

HE.
>   Leave me alone! Don't torment me, don't haunt me.
>   Don't prophesy my dark fate!
>   You celebrate your win!
>   Will you take off your mask? Disappear into the night?

SHE.
>   Come after me! Overtake me!
>   I'm more passionate and mournful than your bride!
>   With your nimble hand, embrace me!
>   Drink of my dark goblet to the bottom!

HE.
>   I pledged my passionate love to another!
>   You flashed your fiery gaze.
>   You led me into a dark alley.
>   You did me in with deadly poison!

SHE.
>   It wasn't I who lured you – my cloak flew
>   In a whirlwind after me – my fiery friend.
>   You yourself wanted to step into
>   The circle of my enchantment.

HE.
>   Watch out, temptress! I'll remove my mask!
>   And you'll find out that I am faceless.
>   You swept away my features, and led me to the darkness,
>   Where my black double nods to me, nods to me.

SHE.
>   I'm a free maiden! My path is toward triumph!
>   Come after me, wherever I lead.
>   Oh, you will follow my fiery trail
>   And you'll be with me in delirium.

HE.
> I'm coming, resigned to my stern fate.
> O, my cloak, my fiery guide, whirl!
> But three of us will go along this ominous road:
> You – and I – and my double.

(They disappear into the whirlwind of cloaks. It seems that after them somebody, a third, utterly akin to the male lover, like the nimble tongue of a black flame, tears loose from the crowd.

A third pair of lovers is revealed amongst those dancing. They sit in the middle of the stage.

The Middle Ages. She follows his movements, leaning back in a reverie. He, all in stern lines, is big and pensive, in a cardboard helmet. He draws a circle on the ground in front of her with a huge, wooden sword.)

HE. Do you understand the play, in which we play not the least role?
SHE. *(Like a soft but distinct echo.)* Role.
HE. Do you know that the maskers have made our meeting today marvelous?
SHE. Marvelous.
HE. So you believe me? O, today you are more beautiful than ever.
SHE. Ever.
HE. You know all that has been and will be. You have understood the meaning of this inscribed circle.
SHE. Circle.
HE. O, how captivating your words are! Sayer of my soul! How much your words say to my heart!
SHE. Heart.
HE. O, Eternal Happiness! Eternal Happiness!
SHE. Happiness.
HE. *(With a sigh of relief and triumph.)* Day is near. The end draws on to this ill-omened night.
SHE. Night.

(At this moment one of the clowns gets it into his head to play a trick. He runs up to the lover and sticks his long tongue out at him. The lover ferociously beats the clown about the head with his heavy wooden sword. The clown leans over the footlights and hangs down. From his head spurts a stream of cranberry juice.)

CLOWN. Help me! I'm hemorrhaging cranberry juice!

(He hangs around a while, then withdraws. Noise. Bustling. Happy shouts: "Torches! Torches! The torch procession!" A chorus appears with torches. The maskers crowd around, smile, jump about.)

CHORUS.
>In the twilight, drop after drop of resin
>Falls with the slightest crackle!
>Faces, hidden by a cloud of haze,
>Are illuminated by a dim sparkle!
>Drop by drop, spark after spark!
>A rain, resinous and clean!
>Where are you, our glittering, quick,
>Fiery leader?

(Harlequin steps out of the chorus as the coryphaeus.)

HARLEQUIN.
>Along streets sleepy and snowy
>I dragged the idiot after me!
>The world was revealed to rebellious orbs.
>A snowy wind sang over me!
>O, how my youthful breast wished
>To breathe in deep and go out into the world,
>To realize in empty isolation,
>My happy springtime feast.
>Here no one dares to understand
>That spring swims at the summit!
>Here no one knows how to love!
>Here they live in mournful slumber!
>Hello, world! You are with me again!
>Your soul has been close to me for so long!
>I'm coming to your golden window
>To breathe in your spring.

(He jumps through the window. The distance, visible through the window, turns out to be painted on paper. The paper rips. Harlequin flies head over heels into the void. In the rip in the paper only the sky, which is turning lighter, can be seen. Night lapses, and morning swarms. Against the background of the breaking morning, slightly trembling in the wind before dawn stands Death in long white shrouds with a dull, feminine face and with a scythe behind her shoulder. The blade turns silver, like the overturned moon dying in the morning.)

Everyone, in horror, rushes in different directions. The knight stumbles over his wooden sword. The ladies drop their flowers all over the stage. The maskers, having flattened up as if crucified against the walls, seem like dolls from an ethnographic museum. The female lovers hide their faces in the cloaks of their lovers. The profile of the blue masker is delicately outlined against the morning sky. At his feet, the frightened, genuflecting pink masker presses her lips to his hand. Popping up from out of nowhere, Pierrot walks slowly across the whole stage, stretching out his hands to Death. As he approaches, Her features begin to come to life. Blush begins to play in her lustreless cheeks. The silver scythe becomes lost in the drifting morning mist. In a bay window, against the background of the dawn, stands Columbine, a beautiful girl with a tranquil smile on her peaceful face. At just the moment when Pierrot walks up to her and wants to touch her hand with his hand – the exultant head of the Author pops up between him and Columbine.)

> AUTHOR. Most esteemed audience! My case is not lost! My rights have been restored! You can see that the obstacles have collapsed! That gentleman fell through the window! You will yet be witnesses to the happy rendezvous of two lovers after a long separation. Even if it cost them much to overcome these obstacles, at least they are now joined together forever!

(The Author wants to unite Columbine and Pierrot's hands. But suddenly all of the scenery rises and flies upward. The maskers run away. The Author remains bent over Pierrot alone, who lies motionlessly on the empty stage in his white overalls with the red buttons.

Having noticed his situation, the Author impetuously runs off.)

> PIERROT. *(Raises himself a little and speaks plaintively and pensively.)*
> Where did you lead? How can I guess?
> You've given me over to fate.
> Poor Pierrot, it's enough to lie and rest.
> Go find yourself a bride.

(Having fallen silent.)

> Oh, how radiant she was, who went away.
> My jingling comrade led her off.
> She fell (from cardboard she was made).
> I came – at her to laugh.

She lay prone and white.
Oh, our dance was fun.
There was no way she could arise.
She was a cardboard bride.

Pale in face, here I stand.
But for you to laugh at me is a sin.
What can I do? She fell prone ...
I'm very sad. You think it's funny?

(Pierrot pensively pulls a flute from his pocket and starts to play a song about his pale face, about his hard life and about his bride, Columbine.)

1906

3. A poster for the production of *The Unknown Woman* and *A Puppet Show* by Vsevolod Meyerhold at the Tenishevsky school auditorium in 1914 Courtesy of Union of Theater Workers' Library, Moscow

CONTEXT OF *A PUPPET SHOW*

RELATED POEMS

A PUPPET SHOW

Look, a puppet show opened
For good, happy kids who behave.
A boy and a girl are hoping
To see kings with their ladies, and devils.
And this music from hell can be heard:
A doleful bow howls.
The devil who has caught a little boy is horrid,
And cranberry juice trickles down.

The Boy
He will be saved from black rage
With a wave or the sleight
Of a white hand. Look: little lights
Are getting nearer and nearer from stage left.
Do you see smoke? Can you see the torchlights?
This is the queen, my favorite.

The Girl
Oh no, why do you tease me?
This is the devil's own retinue . . .
The queen, she comes out in daylight at her ease,
Laced all around with garlands of roses and satinet.
Swords jingle, and her train is upraised
By the knights' lovelorn retinue.

A fool suddenly leans over across the footlights
And shouts: Help!
I'm hemorrhaging cranberry juice!
I'm bandaged with rags!
On my head, there's a helmet of cardboard,
And in my hand, a sword made of wood.

The girl and boy burst into tears,
And the happy puppet show tears to a close.

July 1905

LIGHT STAGGERED IN THE WINDOW

Light staggered in the window.
By the entrance Harlequin
Whispered in the half-gloom,
Alone with the darkness.

His white and red costume
Was shrouded in shadow.
Above – behind the wall –
A fool's masquerade.

There your face was harbored
In a motley lie.
But in your hand could be discerned
An inevitable tremor.

He traced characters
With a wooden sword.
She, by the strangeness enraptured,
Cast her gaze down.

Alone with the darkness,
Not trusting the rapture –
By the pensive door –
Hear Harlequin's laughter.

6 August 1902

HE SHOWED UP AT A WELL-ORDERED BALL

He showed up at a well-ordered ball
In a brilliantly closed circle.
Ill-omened lights were flickering.
His gaze described an arc.

All night they circled in a noisy dance.
All night the circle pressed against the walls.
And in the luster of the window – at dawn,
His noiseless friend appeared.

He stood and raised his owl-like gaze
And watched – intent, alone –
Where jingling Harlequin was running away
Behind his pale-white Columbine.

There in the corner, beneath the icons,
In a crowd that crumples variously,
Rolling his childish eyes,
The deceived Pierrot trembling.

7 October 1902

AT ROUND TABLES, EVERYBODY WAS SCREAMING

At round tables, everybody was screaming,
Changing places excitedly.
From the steam of the wine, it was dim.
Suddenly someone came in and through the voices' din,
Said: "There's my bride!"

Nobody heard anything.
Like beasts, everybody yelped furiously,
But himself not knowing why, one –
He swayed and laughed, pointing at him
And at the girl coming in the door.

She dropped her kerchief,
And all of them, in a striving of spite,
Ripped up every scrap with a squeal, as if
Having understood an ill-omened allusion,
And painted it with blood and dirt.

And when everybody went up to the table again,
Quieted down and sat in their places,
He pointed for them at the girl in the corner
And said in a ringing voice that pierced the gloom:
"Gentlemen! That's my fiancée."

And suddenly the one who had swayed and laughed,
Senselessly stretched out his hands,
Pressed against the table and shuddered –
And those, who before had mindlessly shouted,
Heard weeping sounds.

25 December 1902

YOU WILL DRESS ME IN SILVER

You will dress me in silver,
    And when I expire,
The moon will come out – that Pierrot of the sky.
    In the open, the red fool will arise.

The dead moon is helplessly mute.
    It has opened up nothing to anyone.
It only will ask its girlfriend – why
    Did I care for her once?

In this violent daydream,
    With a dead face, I capsize.
And the fool spooks the owl,
    Jingling his bell down the hill.

I know – his wrinkled-up visage is old
    And shameless in its earthly nakedness.
But the sinister fumes of carbon monoxide rise up –
    To the heavens, the heights, up to purity.

14 May 1904

AT THAT HOUR WHEN NARCISSUSES ARE GETTING DRUNK

At that hour when narcissuses are getting drunk
And the theater is consumed in the fire of sunset,
Sighing about me, someone is walking around
In the half-shadow of the last wing.

Is it Harlequin forgetting his role?
Or you, my quiet-orbed doe?
Or a breeze from the field, bearing
The light tribute of undulation?

I spring up – a clown – in the open
Trap by the shining footlights.
This is – (an abyss looks through the lights) –
An insatiably hungry spider.

And while the narcissuses are getting drunk,
I make faces, jingle and spin.
But someone weeps, feeling sorry for me
In the shadows of the last wing.

With his blue mist, my tender friend
Is lulled by a swing of dreams,
Lonesome, the one who presses to his wounds
The light-fingered scent of flowers.

26 May 1904

A TRAVELLING SHOW

– Well, old nag, let's go
bust up our Shakespeare.
    – Keane[22]

The mist isn't lifting
Above the black mire of the road.
A hearse is groaning, bearing
My faded little show.

The everyday face of Harlequin
Is paler than the visage of Pierrot.
And in the corner, Columbine is hiding
Rags, sewn together in bright colors.

Drag on, funereal nags!
Actors, double check your craft
So everyone starts to feel painful and bright
From our itinerant truth!

Mold penetrated to the cache of the soul,
But you have got to cry, sing, – go
So that well-beaten paths may open
On to the paradise of my seven-sea songs.

---

22 The epigraph is taken from the play *Keane, or Genius and Dissipation* by Alexandre Dumas père. Edmund Keane (1787–1833), British actor renowned for his roles in the Shakespearean repertoire.

4. Fomin's sketch for costumes for a production of *A Puppet Show* in Petrograd, 1920
Courtesy of Union of Theater Workers' Library, Moscow

THE KING ON THE SQUARE

Dramatis Personae

THE KING – on the palace terrace
THE ARCHITECT – an old man in loose and dark clothing. In his features and silver hair, he reminds one of the King
THE DAUGHTER OF THE ARCHITECT – a tall beauty in black silks
THE POET – a youth, guided in his ways by the Architect, and in love with the latter's daughter
A FOOL – a hanger-on of the stage and representative of common sense. Sometimes he conceals his belly, which is embroidered with gold, with a priest's cassock
LOVERS, CONSPIRATORS, COURTIER, A ROSE SELLER, WORKERS, DANDIES, BEGGARS, FACES and VOICES in the crowd
RUMORS – small, red, they rummage around in the city dust

PROLOGUE

(A city square. The background is occupied by the white façade of the palace with its high and wide terrace. On a massive throne – the gigantic King. The crown covers his green, ancient locks, which stream over his tranquil face, furrowed with deep wrinkles. His delicate hands lay on the armrests of the throne. His whole pose is majestic. At the very bottom – by the footlights – under the high parapet of the embankment is a bench. Stairs descend to it from two sides. The bench is on the shore of the sea, which comes in from afar in a thin strip, skirting the cape with the square and the palace from the left, and flowing together with the orchestra and the hall in such a way that the stage represents only an island – a chance refuge for the dramatis personae.

The sun hasn't risen yet. In almost total darkness, the Fool, in the capacity of the Prologue, sails in from the sea, moors his boat at the shore, takes out of it a bundle and a fishing pole, and sits down on the bench.)

FOOL.
The sun still doesn't feel like shining.
    But I am on the shore.
The luminaries can decide whether to labor,
    But I cannot.

But without them, I found my way
    And sailed in here,
So as to mollify you a little, ladies
    And gentlemen, with my good sense.

So here is a palace on the dark background,
    And on the terrace – a throne.
A King, as you see, wears his crown.
    He is old, despondent.

Anyone who wants to rest
    Takes a walk in front of the palace.
Here only a dog or a democrat
    Is not shown the path.

Here is the way for the pure public.
    Here's a bench that's for it.
And I have sat down on it
    Only by right of the Prologue.

In front of me, the sea is in the orchestra.
    Its waves are dark.
But if the sun soon rises,
    I'll see it to its depths.

My duty was just to force you
    To cast your glance on this view.
But common sense is ordering
    Me to angle for fish in roily waters.

(The Fool sits astride the footlights and casts his line into the orchestra pit. During the action of the play, he cannot be seen for the most part behind the side curtain. He appears only in various scenes.)

ACT ONE

Morning

(Night battles with morning. Above the shore, two unknown people are barely visible in the twilight. The First – in black – leans against the white stone of the palace. The other sits on the shore. A Third person cannot be seen: He is somewhere nearby, and only his voice, broken and sinister, can be heard.)

>FIRST. There, the day has started to turn white.
>SECOND. It's excruciating when the day awakens.
>VOICE OF THE THIRD. Don't give in to despair. Don't give in to death.
>FIRST. There's nothing left for me to give in to, comrade. I don't believe in anything anymore. But I fear for the others.
>SECOND and VOICE OF THE THIRD. Don't fear for us.
>FIRST. I don't fear for you. The city terrifies me. All the inhabitants have lost their minds. They build their happiness on some sort of insane dream. They're waiting for something from ships, which are supposed to come today.
>SECOND. *(Grabbing his head.)* My God! My God! Ships from the sea! This is madness! If they believe in this, it means there's nothing left to believe in. What a horrifying time!
>FIRST. It's so easy to say: A horrifying time. If you grant yourself the will, anybody will go crazy. Let's find the strength in ourselves to live this day to the end so that we can die then.
>SECOND. What happiness – to die!
>VOICE OF THE THIRD. He talks about happiness. Let's go alone to burn and destroy.
>FIRST. Let him talk. That's nothing. His despair is also immeasurable.

(They are silent.)

>SECOND. Neither shelter, nor family. There's nowhere to lay my head. It's terrifying.
>FIRST. He who feels sorry for nothing has nothing to fear.
>SECOND. Twilight towards dawn. Mortal anguish.
>VOICE OF THE THIRD. Burn. Burn.
>SECOND. It's terrifying. I feel sorry.
>VOICE OF THE THIRD. Die if you're sorry.

(They are silent. It slowly grows light out.)

SECOND. Tell me, friend, you once believed in virtue, didn't you?

FIRST. I'll shake on that. I sought well-being too. I too loved those domestic comforts, where it smelled like perfume, where a woman put bread and flowers on the table.

SECOND. Did you love children?

FIRST. Let's drop this. I loved children. But I'm not even sorry for the children anymore.

SECOND. Tell me one last thing: Do you believe that destruction is liberating?

FIRST. I don't.

SECOND. Thanks. I don't either.

(They are silent.)

FIRST. *(Looks at the King.)* There he slumbers over us. The beauty of his ancient locks rules the world. For could such decrepit hands rule the world?

SECOND. You're afraid of something. We are strong only with your strength. But if even you are a phantom, then we will wane in this vagrant morning light. People won't follow us. The people fear deceit.

FIRST. Everybody will follow us. The hour will arrive, and everybody will follow us.

SECOND. They have their families, their houses.

FIRST. Their families have been corrupted. Their houses lean to one side.

SECOND. There's no place for fire in them.

FIRST. Just the same, everything will burn. The heavy and the light, the dry and the damp. There's just more smoke from the damp.

SECOND. And will the old man be consumed?

FIRST. There's nothing left in him to burn. Everything turned to stone.

SECOND. So he'll remain untouched!

VOICE OF THE THIRD. We'll scatter him to the wind. We'll throw him into the sea.

SECOND. Won't anyone remember him?

FIRST. Whoever loved him will remember him.

(They are silent. The day flames up.)

FIRST. In the whole city I know only two living people. Everybody fears the old Architect.

SECOND. Do you fear him too?

FIRST. No, he won't interfere with us. The crowd is too petty to obey the will of a titan.

SECOND. Who's the other one?
FIRST. The other one? His daughter.
SECOND. That's hilarious! You're afraid of a woman? Your voice trembled!
FIRST. Don't laugh. I'm not afraid of good sense, or will, or labor, or coarse masculine strength. But I am afraid of a reckless fantasy, of nonsense, of what is sometimes called the lofty dream.
SECOND. You're afraid of religion, poetry? The world stepped past them long ago. The world has forgotten about prophets and poets.
FIRST. That's the way it was. But at their hour of death everyone recalls the sublime, that which had been forgotten. She will infect them with her reckless beauty. Invisibly and mysteriously, she rules the city now. She wants to breathe new life into the king.
SECOND. Is that really possible? Will that really halt the destruction?
FIRST. Yes. They will prostrate themselves before her. They will make her their queen. They will start to bow before her in temples.
SECOND. The old dreams aren't being resurrected.
FIRST. But everybody is ready to go back to the old madnesses. They are capable of crowning their own madness, when all hope and all virtue has been lost.
SECOND. You're raving mad. You've lost your mind.
FIRST. So be it. You are powerless without me. Believe me, her father's creative intoxication and the rage of the last several generations are in her.
SECOND. What can we do?
FIRST. Wait this day out. This evening she'll be talking with the people and the king.
SECOND. Another whole day? Empty and light? It would be better to die.
FIRST. I swear: We will all die toward nightfall.
VOICE OF THE THIRD. (*Like an echo.*) We will die.

(*It is broad daylight. The city wakes up – the music of morning noises is all the more audible. From far off, from the seaside, the wind bears the pounding of axes.*)

SECOND. Do you hear that? They still haven't lost hope. Their little axes pound.
FIRST. They pound, and they build. They'll be building until the last moment.
SECOND. They're decorating the pier. They're erecting some kind of structure for meeting the ships.

FIRST. Let them hope. We alone will perish if the ships arrive, or if her lofty dream is realized.
VOICE OF THE THIRD. The ships won't come. The storm will destroy them. A hot wind spreads death.

(They disperse. The Third emerges from behind the stone. In the dry features of his face and his bony body he is, more than anything, like a bird. On the square in front of the palace, people start walking by. Several dandies pass to and fro. Two workers, late for work, walk in.)

FIRST WORKER. Work has begun. Come along quickly.
SECOND WORKER. Yesterday one of them came to talk with us. He forbade us to build. He said the storm would shatter everything.

(They pass by in a hurry. The wind chases little streams of dust. A pale woman is selling roses. A Youth and a Girl stop not far from her.)

GIRL.
    Lift up your gaze to the heavens.
    The sunny day will alleviate all of your sorrow.
YOUTH.
    Clouds are swimming and swimming eternally.
    They drop their white towers down into the seas.
GIRL.
    You are sad. Look into my eyes.
    Read the joy of my meeting with you.
YOUTH.
    I see that your eyes have turned blue.
    Towards nightfall your youth will draw you on.
GIRL.
    Let's be happy! Let's be happy! The seas are singing!
    I can hear the ships coming from far, far away.
YOUTH.
    I can hear the distant waves murmur.
    I can see the wind chase the clouds.
GIRL.
    The beams of the lighthouses penetrate mists.
    Over the pier they'll place lights as precaution.
YOUTH.
    Look – the storm petrels are roving over the foam.
    On the crest of a wave, fate pitches them.
GIRL.
    A gold rocket will fly up above the storm
    To greet my glad ships!

YOUTH.
>I penetrate with prophetic soul those melodies
>Which promise us inescapable night.

GIRL.
>That pale woman has fragrant roses –
>The innocent pledge of a tranquil day.

(Goes up to the Seller of Roses.)

GIRL. Why are you pale? And why are you staggering?
SELLER OF ROSES. I'm dying from the hot sun, from the dust, from weariness, from hunger.
GIRL. You're dying?
SELLER OF ROSES. I will suffocate you with flowers if you don't give me some bread.
GIRL. *(Gives money.)* Give me some roses. Leave as quickly as you can.

(Seller of Roses leaves.)

GIRL. A starving woman! The morning has perished.

(Two dandies meet up above.)

FIRST DANDY. Tell me why is it they are so expectantly awaiting these ships?
SECOND DANDY. Indeed, I myself do not know. Isn't it all the same after all?
FIRST DANDY. I am glad to meet a sensible person. Everyone is so excited. They talk of nothing other than the ships. And you know, you yourself start to believe.
SECOND DANDY. Yes, whatever you say, the influence of the crowd can't be denied. It's infectious.
FIRST DANDY. And the more reckless, the more infectious.
SECOND DANDY. The time has come to take energetic measures and disperse these rumors. The government . . .

(They pass by.)

GIRL.
>How pathetic these snippets of speech of the sated are.
>How frightening the flowers the beggars have in their hands are.
>I don't believe in my ships anymore.

YOUTH.
>Don't think about them anymore.
>>Look at the flowers.

GIRL.
>I can't breathe because of white flowers!

YOUTH.
>Let's forget the flowers. Look in my eyes.
>These heavy roses are burning you up.

GIRL.
>I'll throw them into the sea. Let's forget about them.

(They go down to the sea.)

GIRL.
>Let's forget what is frightening.
>Let's recall what we love.
>Drift, drift, drift, flowers.

(She throws the roses in the water. With a sad gaze, the Youth follows the easy movements of his beloved.)

ACT TWO

Midday

(The same scenery, only the colors have lost their luster, and the lines have been burnt out by the intense heat. The sea is motionless. The horizon is lost in haze. There are a few people strolling on the square. Workers and bums sometimes pass by at the side. Axes faintly, but persistently, pound in the distance.)

>FIRST WORKER. They're waiting for the ships from hour to hour.
>SECOND WORKER. I'd like to know what they expect from them. They hurry to build the structure, and they make us sing songs so that we work more happily.
>FIRST WORKER. They build, and they build, but they haven't finished building.

(They go by. From far off comes the doleful song of the workers. In come two dandies.)

>FIRST DANDY. Someone said that the ships are already visible from the pier.
>SECOND DANDY. A false rumor! Those are fishing vessels skirting the cape.
>FIRST DANDY. What difference does it make? They take these ships too much to heart. Who thought up all this nonsense, I'd like to know?

(They pass on. The Fool wanders in with his fishing pole in hand.)

>FOOL. Rotten weather. Even the fish aren't biting. Nobody wants to go for the hook of common sense. Everybody's lost their mind. At last, here come the very craziest – perchance something will bite!

(Goes behind the curtain. The Architect and the Poet sit down on the bench.)

>POET. Nobody sleeps at night anymore. There's alarm in every face. Everybody's waiting for something. Teach me to fight with anguish.
>ARCHITECT. You yourself don't know what your alarm is about.
>POET. If only I knew! A starving man procures bread through labor. The humiliated seek revenge. A lover says to a woman: Be mine. But I am full, and nobody insults me. In women I love only fine

tresses, melodious voices, and a dream of the impossible. There's nothing left for me to attain – I am doomed to anguish.

(The workers' song is barely audible.)

ARCHITECT. Know that your alarm is in vain. Don't think about the impossible. As long as the sea washes the shore, as long as the king rules the city, nothing will change, besides your stray thoughts.
POET. Consciousness keeps me from living. I know that the city's life is just as spectral as mine. The sea seems to me made of glass, the people seem dolls.
ARCHITECT. You're ill.
POET. It often seems to me that the king too . . .
ARCHITECT. *(Interrupting.)* You're sick. Live more simply. You are a poet, a senseless singing being; however, you are fated to express the thoughts of others. They just don't know how to state everything that you say. Woe to you, if you prompt the people with their own secret, crazy thoughts.

(A distant crash and shouts, as if something heavy had fallen into the water. Workers come running across the square.)

WORKER. The scaffolding tore loose. Ten people fell into the sea!
ANOTHER WORKER. A family without bread!
THIRD WORKER. Tell his wife to run to the sea: Maybe it's still possible to save him.
POET. Today, I feel that something unheard of is about to take place. The air is too hot. My soul is too empty.
ARCHITECT. Do you think the world will overturn? Perhaps you too await the ships?
POET. *(Enthusiastically.)* The ships will come!
ARCHITECT. Madman! You castigate their families. You castigate their vulgarity. But they are all better than you. You are affected. You can't breathe the sea or the dust. They, at least, know how to breathe the yellow, stinking dust. Bend down before them on your knees!
POET. You're killing me.
ARCHITECT. Wretch! Perhaps too many beggars have come crawling from distant quarters today, and they've upset the nerves of the fine ladies and gentlemen with the twang of their voices. Perhaps too many children have died, and their mothers are crying too loudly. Perhaps hot wind has simply spread rumors and gossip across the city. There – that's all your anguish is.
POET. Stop. You're killing in the last . . .

ARCHITECT. There's your end of the world. Somewhere dogs are fighting, or women are gossiping and screeching! And you're dreaming about the final day! They will labor, hunger, and die right next to you, but you'll come to from your delirium only towards evening.

(The pounding of the axes starts up again.)

POET. Your words pound like axes into my heart.
ARCHITECT. I'm not taking hope away from you. But think about what I've said. Listen, listen to the axes pounding – Let them beat you all the more painfully. Otherwise your heart will grow lifeless and empty. I will turn away from you. I trust only those who distinguish between good and evil. Goodbye.

(He leaves. A gust of wind flaps his loose clothing. A cloud of yellow dust carpets the square, the palace, and the King. One can see little red Rumors darting out of clouds of dust. They jump around and scatter in every direction. It seems that the wind is whistling when they laugh merrily. At this precise moment, alarmed voices in the crowd of strollers can be heard.)

VOICES IN THE CROWD. The King is sick! Near death!
The conspirators want to burn down the palace!
The King has been taken into custody!
They deceived us! Is that really the King?

(The dust has lifted. As before, the palace and the tranquil figure of the King can be seen. The crowd quiets down. Those out for a stroll continue on their way. At the same time refreshing breezes blow by in the air, as if the heat were sleeping. The Architect's Daughter, a tall beauty in tight black silks, emerges from the crowd slowly, but with a light step. She stops at the edge, right under the bench where the Poet, who is wasted by his anguish, sits. She looks at him from above.)

ARCHITECT'S DAUGHTER. Do you hear me?
POET. *(Looks up.)* I hear music. The smell of salt comes up from the sea.

(The wind has ceased, and the pounding of the axes has grown still. For some time one can hear the distant music of the sea, which the Fool's grumbling interrupts.)

FOOL. It has started. A big fish just nibbled. But fools in love will scare away all my fish.

(Silence. As the Architect's Daughter slowly descends, the stage is clouded over by mist, which leaves visible only the little island of the bench, where the Architect's Daughter and the Poet find themselves.)

ARCHITECT'S DAUGHTER.
    When the dust settles down
    And red Rumors have hidden themselves
    In their burrows at noon,
    This music is born in the sea.
    The Soul is refreshed under the wind.
POET.
    There descends a transparent mist
    That dwindles as white infatuation,
    But the primordial sea cannot
    Muffle the piercing voice
    Of the Fool with its melody.
ARCHITECT'S DAUGHTER.
    You speak as in sleep.
    I know your soul's singing
    And love your dark speeches.
POET.
    All I can speak is the vague.
    Ineffable are the soul's legends.

(The sea sighs, dragging out a mist.)

POET.
    In the distance a white sail wanes.

ARCHITECT'S DAUGHTER.
    You are filled with my vision.

POET.
    In the distance I can see the ships, the ships . . .

ARCHITECT'S DAUGHTER.
    I cast this spell – be true.

POET.
    I see the shore of a new land . . .

ARCHITECT'S DAUGHTER.
    I remove the spell. You're free.

(It's as if the wind had blown, and the mist had moved. The milky whiteness is already no longer there. The sun breaks through from somewhere. But still, only the bench is visible.)

POET.
    The spray of the sea foam blinded me.
    You move, above the sea,
    And the shadow of the ships rises after you.
ARCHITECT'S DAUGHTER.
    With your child-like soul, you're truer than anyone to me.
    You'll sing when I'm with you,
    And when I perish, you'll sing.
POET.
    Be with me! My wings grow!
    I'm weak when the crowd rages.
    I'm weak when your father speaks.
    My heart is open to you alone.
    My soul is devoted to dark melodies.

(The silence is again broken by the peevish voice of the Fool.)

FOOL. Indeed, this is all old hat. No matter what she says, he will like it because he is an infatuated idiot. Of course, he would never listen to that old grump, her father.

(The Fool climbs out from behind the curtain. His loathsome profile with his fishing pole hides the lovers from the hall for a moment. Then he goes up the staircase and is lost in the mist.)

POET.
    My anguish is dressed in the mist's silver chasuble.
ARCHITECT'S DAUGHTER.
    The day's sunbeams have pierced the mist's heart.
POET.
    The voice of anguish rings out.
ARCHITECT'S DAUGHTER.
    That's the waves speaking hoarsely by the shore.
POET.
    How clear the piercing voice of anguish is.
ARCHITECT'S DAUGHTER.
    The sun will pierce its chasuble and its heart –
                    You will be free.
POET.
    The sun will set soon.

ARCHITECT'S DAUGHTER.
   At sunset, you will be free.
POET.
   Your tales of freedom captivate me.
ARCHITECT'S DAUGHTER.
   The tale is all of life for you.
   Listen with your sleepy soul
   To the tale of life in the evening,
   You, who are enchanted by me.
POET.
   Yes, speak, my princess,
   In such a way that vivid dreams
   Flow before me,
   Vivid dreams of a land that has never been.
ARCHITECT'S DAUGHTER.
   I know a great book about a light country,
   Where a beautiful maiden went up
   To the death bed of the tsar
   And breathed youth into his decrepit heart!
   There – above the blossoming land
   Rules the majestic King!
   Youth has returned to him!

(During the preceding scene, the sea sings more and more loudly. In the course of the last words, the mist dissipates entirely, and dust, in which red Rumors dart about, begins to sift. The sound of axes again carries distinctly through the growing din of the crowd gathered by the palace.)

ARCHITECT'S DAUGHTER.
   Life left for a moment,
   But it has returned again.
   Do you hear how some build?
   Do you hear how the others are murmuring?
   Do you see how the Rumors are stirring the crowd?
POET.
   Your visions are alien. Your words too are alien.
   I am breathing your tale.
   Don't leave me.
ARCHITECT'S DAUGHTER.
   No, I cannot remain here with you!
   I must incarnate my legend.
   Await me towards evening here.
   Be true to the king in your soul.
   You'll be free towards evening.

(She goes up and mixes in with the crowd, which murmurs hollowly in clouds of dust. The Poet, pensive, remains below.)

>VOICES IN THE CROWD. Did you hear that the ships came in the night!
>The King nodded his head today . . .
>The King issued the order! The ships went back!
>Look up: the King is no longer there!
>The King is here! You can't see anything in this dust!

(The voices are cut off by strange sounds – as if someone were sobbing. Through the dust one can make out the Fool, who clings with his belly to the parapet of the embankment, above the bench itself, and covers his mouth with both hands to hold back his laughter.)

>FOOL. *(Yells through the din.)* Your grace! How may I be of service?
>POET. *(Arising quickly, looks up at the Fool.)* I've seen you already in my sleep. Where's your fishing pole?
>FOOL. *(Guffaws from laughter.)* Here it is, here it is, right here with me. I'm a fisher of men!
>POET. Help me! Rescue me from anguish.
>FOOL. While you were having your little talk, a whole political revolution was prepared here.
>POET. Are the ships near?
>FOOL. What ships? Have you lost your marbles? Join the party! You can't just dawdle around with nothing to do!
>POET. What's to be done? Tell me!
>FOOL. Hurry up and choose. I brought two along for your selection.

(From behind the Fool's back two, who are similar to birds, lean out from either side: One is in black, the other in gold. They run down to the Poet.)

>BLACK ONE. It's time. Follow us! Sing our songs. The city languishes without songs!
>POET. Who are you?
>BLACK ONE. Don't lose any time! Sing of freedom! The crowd is agitated – It will follow you.
>POET. You're against the King?
>BLACK ONE. Death to him!
>POET. Go away. She won't allow you to touch what's sacred.

(The Black One runs off cursing.)

>FOOL. *(Yells.)* Talk with the other one!

(The crowd drones. The Golden One bows to the Poet.)

> GOLDEN ONE. I'm happy to speak with you. Don't lose a minute. The crowd is in your hands.
> POET. Who are you, golden bird?
> GOLDEN ONE. The King's loyal servant. A courtier. Your admirer.
> POET. What can I do?
> GOLDEN ONE. Sing of the sacred. Preserve the King from the violent rabble. Every instant is precious.
> POET. I will sing. Lead on.

(Quickly goes up. The Golden One skips on ahead. The crowd drones on.)

> FOOL. *(Guffawing from laughter.)* I caught one! I caught one! At least one with common sense! Non-party! A government sympathizer!

(The Fool mixes in with the crowd. The Poet, going up above the crowd on one of the steps of the terrace, speaks amidst the quieting popular storm:

> POET. It's all as if in a dream.

(He turns to face the crowd. It is silent and ready to hearken to his songs.)

ACT THREE

Night

(The same scenery. Evening is coming on. Leaden clouds run across the sky. The intensified pounding of axes carries from afar. Across the stage, without interruption, people go to the sea, skirting the palace. Their gestures are animated, and their eyes glisten. Their agitation has reached an extreme degree. There is alarm and greedy hope in every face. One from the crowd stops and leans on the railing of the embankment. A Second joins him.)

SECOND. You've grown completely weak.
FIRST. Yes, this insane anxiety has taken its toll. My heart won't hold out if this continues for even one more day. Can it be that the ships won't arrive today either?
SECOND. They have to be here today. Otherwise – we've perished. The people are certain that the ships will bring salvation. If they don't come today either, their patience will be exhausted.
FIRST. The final, final hours! Look, they're all going to the pier, and they'll wait until nightfall. What if they don't wait it out?
SECOND. A storm will chase them into their homes.
FIRST. A storm will only provoke them. All night they will burn and plunder. Then, everything will end.
SECOND. Who engendered this hope in us? Only the preparations for a solemn greeting, and promises of eternal happiness.
FIRST. *(Leaning low on the railing.)* I have moments of enlightenment. As before death. Where does it take us? What made us believe?
SECOND. Only our grabbing onto life. To believe in this means to grasp at straws.
FIRST. The axes, the axes pound. They pound without rest. Where can you escape from the pounding of the axes?
SECOND. They pound from morning to evening. They're building a tower to shoot off a rocket when the first ship appears in the sea.
FIRST. *(Weeps.)* My knees are giving out! I haven't slept for so many nights! Rest! Rest!
SECOND. Be patient. Maybe we won't have long to wait.

(There is no answer. The First leans low on the railing. At this moment a Beggarwoman with a child in her arms approaches.)

BEGGARWOMAN. Help us for the love of God. My husband drowned at sea. Give us something for bread.

(*The Second, not paying attention to her, looks intently into the face of the First. The latter has slumped completely down on the railing and let his head hang down. People walk past.*)

BEGGARWOMAN. Good people, help us for the sake of the child.

(*Silence.*)

BEGGARWOMAN. Everyone will be happy today. The ships will come. Only I will be without bread.

(*The child starts to cry. The Beggarwoman rocks him, stepping away with surprise. The Second embraces the First, who has slumped down on the railing, in his arms. The body falls to its knees. The deceased's head lies on the iron crossbar.*)

SECOND. (*Sinking down over the corpse, he speaks quietly to the Beggarwoman.*) He died. Listen. The dead don't give alms.

(*The Beggarwoman crosses herself, backs up, and leaves. People walk past. Amongst them is the Fool in a priest's chasuble and cowl. With curiosity, he approaches the corpse, above which the Second helplessly bends.*)

FOOL. Drunk?
SECOND. (*Seriously.*) Dead.
FOOL. Cause of death?
SECOND. Rupture of the heart. The anxious events of these days.
FOOL. (*Shaking his head.*) Everything could have turned out satisfactorily, if he had turned to me.
SECOND. Who exactly are you?
FOOL. A doctor of the spirit.

(*A gust of wind flings open his chasuble and tears the cowl from the Fool's head.*)

SECOND. (*Shakes his head doubtfully.*) A spiritual doctor doesn't wear a red cap. A spiritual doctor doesn't hang gold lace on his red belly . . .

(*The Fool's cheeks quiver from laughter. He quickly draws his chasuble together. Evening comes on quietly.*)

FOOL. (*Severely.*) Even you are laughing? You're laughing when your friend has just died?

(A small group of people from the passing crowd gathers around them. Everyone tries to get a closer look out of curiosity.)

> SECOND. *(Looks at the Fool with wonder.)* I've seen your ugly, sanctimonious mug somewhere. I don't remember – I've seen a lot in my time: In the court, where you inspired the jury with death sentences; or in the church, where you preached humility; or . . . yes! here, on the shore, you tried to prove to the people that they didn't need freedom.

(Hate awakens on the faces of those surrounding them.)

> FOOL. Brethren, mournful events are happening here. Go your own way. Calm down. In the name of God . . .
> VOICES IN THE CROWD. A new lie! Don't use the Lord's name in vain! Truth! Truth! A cunning heart hides under that chasuble!

(The Fool instantly flings open his chasuble. It's as if he's grown into red and gold clothes. His fool's cap sways above the crowd.)

> FOOL. You need the truth? Here's your truth! Gather around, people! Look upon me from the rooftops! Greet me in the streets! Bow down to the ground before me!

(A terrible agitation runs through the crowd that is there. The Fool shakes his cap. The bells jingle.)

> VOICES IN THE CROWD. Maskers in the streets on such a night!
>   – Where are we? Where are we?
>   – Night is near!
> FOOL. You need the truth? It is before you, people! Look upon me! I am Truth itself in its red and gold nakedness! Gather the corpses from your streets!
> VOICES IN THE CROWD. It's horrible!
>   – This specter over the dead man! The wind sends apparitions!
>   – Rumors have been rushing around in the dust all day long!
>   – The little ones have been spinning under our legs. The red ones have been yelling in our ears. And the dusty ones have spread alarm!
>   – Rumors possess the crowd!
>   – This is one of them! Look how fat he's gotten towards nightfall!
>   – Night is near!
>   – This is the voice of the people. This is the common word! The wind bears it over the whole earth! Hearken to it! Hearken to it!

FOOL. I am the word of the people! I have many faces, but in the whole universe, I bear only one name! Common Sense is my name!

VOICES. Listen! Common Sense is speaking with us!

FOOL. Poor sheep without a shepherd! Let your heart calm down! I am a good shepherd! Don't tarry over the place where you can smell grief! This anxious night will pass! Don't tarry – return to your abandoned families!

VOICES. We believe you! Our hearts are open! Speak!

FOOL. I will shepherd you, my flock, with an iron staff! If you do not obey me, terrible punishment will befall you! The sea will overflow the madmen! The leaden clouds will bury beneath them a city in disarray! Thus spake Common Sense! He punishes those who are rebellious in their souls! My red gold sings happily before you! But, should you test Common Sense, my happy red gold will bring you death and conflagration!

VOICES. Quiet! Calm down! It's frightening! Woe to the madman! Let's go! To the sea! To the sea! Let's meet the ships!

(The crowd rustles and breaks up. They carry out the deceased. Individual exclamations die out. The Fool, having wrapped himself in his chasuble, again makes his away through the crowd. Soon no one remains on the stage. The stragglers hurriedly pass by on their way to the pier, where the pounding of the axes has fallen silent.

The Architect appears on the square.)

ARCHITECT. They are finishing their project.

(He stands in the middle of the square and looks at the King. The Poet slowly comes out from the right, heading after the crowd toward the sea.)

ARCHITECT. Even you are following the crowd?

POET. From time immemorial you have barred my way, though our city devours and divides everybody.

ARCHITECT. Yes, the city knocks everybody off their track. But it is easy for me to find the road, for I am alien to you all. You look greedily into each other's eyes. I look over your heads and see my sky-blue path clearly.

POET. They call you a sorcerer. Various Rumors circulate about you.

ARCHITECT. Little Rumors will be the ruin of you. They are born in the dry and yellow dust; and together with it, they penetrate rebellious hearts. A heavenly storm will descend and flatten the dust, and you will perish together with the dust.

(The Architect looks at the swirling clouds.)

>POET. I don't want to see you anymore. I wanted to learn from you of your wisdom, but you are proud and old. You don't love me.
>ARCHITECT. You wouldn't have met me, if I didn't love you.
>POET. *(Wringing his hands.)* What can I do?
>ARCHITECT. Remain here. Don't follow after the crowd. Don't sing rebel songs for it. I enjoin you to remain through the night. May he be saved, who pronounces words of love on such a night.

(The Architect withdraws. The Poet goes down to the sea and sits on the bench. Twilight quickly closes in. The wind's horn trumpets; the dust swirls; the storm approaches; the crowd rumbles hollowly in the distance, on the pier, from whence signal lights are visible. Up above the bench appears the Architect's Daughter. The wind plays in her black hair, in the midst of which her bright visage is as day.)

>POET.
>>I hear, I hear your approach.
>>Again you arise above the dust,
>>Like a vision, momentary.
>>You will vanish in the new dust.
>>A new wind will bear you away.
>
>ARCHITECT'S DAUGHTER.
>>I come down to you for the last time.
>>Bad news has reached me.
>>Shreds of new plans rush about
>>Like black birds, in the yellow dust.
>
>POET.
>>Night draws near.
>>Above the sea, dusk grows ruddy.
>>Leaden clouds rush by.
>>Slumbering youth has awakened in me.
>
>ARCHITECT'S DAUGHTER.
>>The mirror of the seas has been smashed by the wind!
>>The sea has spilled over in your soul!
>>Do you hear the cry of ill-omened birds?
>>Do you hear the splash of the leaden waves?

(The wind rends her black silks and tosses in her hair. The gloom thickens.)

POET.
> At this ill-omened hour, at this last hour, perhaps,
> Let me press my lips to your hand.
> It is white beneath the black clouds.

ARCHITECT'S DAUGHTER.
> Touch my hand for the last time.

POET.
> I know you for the first time tonight.

ARCHITECT'S DAUGHTER.
> You see me for the last time.

POET.
> Why did youth blaze up so brightly?
> Will life really burn out so soon?
> Has youth really passed, my princess?

ARCHITECT'S DAUGHTER.
> I have power over your life.
> Whoever is with me will be free.
> Don't call me princess.
> I am the daughter of the mad crowd!

POET.
> This is how the autumn wind whistled.
> This is the way the dust flew in clouds.
> When for the first time I saw
> Your strange and delicate image.

ARCHITECT'S DAUGHTER.
> I searched for a hero in you.
> I'm looking the future in the eyes.

POET.
> You came down to me from high chambers.
> You were looking, as you are looking now, at the sunset!

ARCHITECT'S DAUGHTER.
> There is no past.

(Pale lightning.)

POET.
> But the wind played in dreamy outlines,
> And before you, I was a luminous poet,
> Covered by your wind.
> And in your lowered eyes
> I read that I am loved by you.

ARCHITECT'S DAUGHTER.
> Forget about the past. There is no past.

POET.
>   But you touched me with your hand!
>   I pressed my lips to this hand!
>   The crown of a princess blazed
>   In your dark hair.

ARCHITECT'S DAUGHTER.
>   I never was a princess!
>   And how would I know splendor?
>   I am the poor daughter of the crowd.

POET.
>   For the last time – in the savage gloom –
>   I see – the crown of a princess burns
>   In your dark hair!
>   Or did the light of a lightningbolt slide by?
>   How your face has lit up!

(In the pale light of a lightningbolt, it seems that her black silks shine. In her dark hair blazes a crown. She suddenly embraces him ... The growing howl of the crowd that has arrived carries from distant quarters, from distant squares. It seems the stormy night itself has choked with this howl, with this whistle of the tempest, with this sobbing of the waves, which beat against the shore in trembling, dull brilliance that is sated by the thunderstorm.)

ARCHITECT'S DAUGHTER. *(Suddenly straightening up, she pushes him away.)*
>   Do you see how the sea hurls itself ashore?
>   Do you see the icon lamps of the lightningbolts have caught fire?
>   The brethren await me! Farewell!

(He remains alone in the impenetrable gloom between the surf of the sea and the crowd which gushes onto the square above him.

She ascends the steps and steps onto the square. A wild howl.)

PERSON WITH A TORCH. *(Rushes around in the crowd and yells on the run, as if caught up by the wind.)* They gave the sign from the pier! Somebody saw a ship from the tower!

(New torches appear, spreading a smoky, reddish light. A tall Figure in Black is on the terrace steps.)

PERSON IN BLACK. You are all gathered here. Night approaches. The last deadlines, which were designated by you for the arrival of these hapless ships, have run out.

(A roar and a screech in the crowd.)

>And there – there are no ships! Beware, you who are starving! Beware, you who suffer! They'll deceive you again! They'll promise you impossible happiness. Vengeance to the one who looks on your destruction indifferently! My insulted people, it is in your hands! There he is, above my head!

(He raises his hand, pointing at the King. The crowd rips the air apart with its wail. At this moment the Architect's Daughter appears next to the black figure. She stands silently and motionlessly looks at the crowd.)

>VOICE IN THE CROWD. Sorceress! Why has she come?

(Suddenly a woman's wailing bursts through: Holy one!*)*

>OTHER VOICES. *(Catching each other up, they gather momentum across the square.)* You are our defense! Heal our wounds! Free us! Help us! Give us new life!

(The black figure of the conspirator disappears. The Architect's Daughter slowly ascends the steps to the terrace. The crowd quiets.)

>SOMEONE'S VOICE. *(Too ordinary to hear him clearly. He says:)* Examples are known in history when women . . . I would not be surprised . . .

(The Fool's red cap flashes somewhere in the crowd, and his restrained laughter, covered by hissing, is audible. The Architect's Daughter appears on the terrace and stops a few steps away from the King. The crowd is completely silent. Above the city, which is as if dead from the enthusiasm of anticipation, tower only these two: She and the King.)

>SHE. *(Breaks the silence in a low voice that issues from her chest. Her voice slowly carries from above, like the sigh of church bells.)* King! The future is in my hands. Your people have given me your power over them.

(Silence.)

>King! There is enough power in me now to smite you down. No one will cry over your old dust if my will is carried out.

(Silence. Her voice becomes brighter and more alarmed, like a fire flaming up for the last time.)

> King! I don't want to kill you. If your fire burns out, that fire of the narrow strip of sunset goes out too. I can do more than extinguish light. I return to you your former strength and give back to you your former power. There – I give you my untouched body, King! Take it so that youth catches fire in your ancient mind from my youth.

(The silence is not violated by a single sound. The red strip of sunset pales. The Architect's Daughter moves forward. At a remove of a single stride from the King, she kneels down and presses her lips to the King's mantle, which lays in folds on the ground.

She arises with a pale face and speaks hoarsely from above.)

> ARCHITECT'S DAUGHTER. Don't touch him. Let him doze and gaze on the stars. I recognized in him the stamp of the Father.

(Tranquil, she sits down at his feet with a submissive motion, having embraced his gigantic knees. She seems a child now at the feet of the regal Father. The crowd is all the same enchanted. Surprised whispers carry back and forth. Women quietly weep. The Fool, with fishing pole and bundle, picks his way through the crowd toward the sea. His red cap quavers from the wind.)

> FOOL. *(Mumbles.)* I said the sea was too roily today. No one here needs me anymore. Who will listen to Common Sense when everybody's lost their heads? Just wait, you'll miss me, it will be too late. For the time being, there remains only one means for Common Sense – emigration.

(Goes down to the sea and goes off into the gloom to look for his boat. A child cries. A mother, a beggarwoman, rocks him frightenedly, but the crying does not fall silent. Then the Beggarwoman screeches piercingly, raising the child above the crowd.)

> BEGGARWOMAN. My child is dying!
> VOICE OF A BEGGAR. *(Joins in.)* Help us! I'm dying . . .
> MANY VOICES. Bread! They've deceived us! Down with the King! Down with the palace!
> THE SAME ORDINARY VOICE. You can't feed people with

fantasies. It's time to do the deed yourself when the powers-that-be don't act.

(Confusion. From the direction of the sea, people come running onto the stage. The Golden One runs swiftly ahead.)

> GOLDEN ONE. *(Yells.)* The ships have arrived! Happiness! Happiness!

(In the distance, a rocket flies up, and after it, another. Rockets fly more and more often.)

> VOICES IN THE CROWD. It's too late! Too late!

(The Black One, bony as a bird, darts out onto the terrace steps.)

> BLACK ONE. Common Sense has abandoned us! Look, you have neither food nor shelter. You're in the power of Rumors. Golden and red devils rush about amongst you! Burn, destroy everything. You can't guarantee tomorrow!

(From below the Poet appears out of the gloom. His ecstatic face glows above the square. For one moment he stops amongst the crowd.)

> POET. Happiness is with us! The ships have arrived! I'm free!

(He begins his final ascent upon the terrace steps. The fury of the crowd mounts with his every step. With every step, the Architect's Daughter greets him from above with her gaze.)

> POET. *(Going up.)* Heavenly rose! I'm coming to you!
> ARCHITECT'S DAUGHTER. *(At the King's feet.)* You're going to the Father.
> POET. *(Higher.)* Look, the rockets fall like rain – petals of heavenly roses!
> ARCHITECT'S DAUGHTER. You're free.
> POET. *(Still higher.)* Your face is illumined!
> ARCHITECT'S DAUGHTER. Closer! Closer!
> POET. *(On the last step.)* Greetings, heaven!
> ARCHITECT'S DAUGHTER. Higher! Higher! Passing me, you go to the Father!

(At that moment, the infuriated crowd bursts onto the steps after the Poet. Columns are loosened from below. Howling and shouts. The terrace is

destroyed, taking with it the King, the Poet, the Architect's Daughter and part of the people. One can clearly see how below people dig in the red light of torches, looking for corpses. They raise a stone fragment of the mantle, a stone piece of torso, a stone hand. Cries of horror are heard: "A statue! – A stone idol! – Where is the King?".)

> ARCHITECT. (*Appears above a mound of fragments and waits motionlessly until the crowd falls silent.*) I sent you my beloved son, and you killed him. I sent you another comforter – my daughter. And you didn't spare her. I created power for you. I hewed the hard marble – and everyday you admired the beauty of these ancient locks, which were fashioned by my chisel. You smashed my creation, and there your house is left empty. But tomorrow the world will be green as before, and the sea just as tranquil.
> VARIOUS FADING VOICES. Who will feed us? Who will return our husbands and children to us? Who will still our pain?
> ARCHITECT. He, Who moves the luminaries, will feed you; He, Who waters the black earth with rains; He, Who gathers clouds over the sea. The Father will feed you.

(He slowly descends from the fragment of the palace and vanishes in the gloom. Behind this picture of destruction, there is no longer even a single light. A pale gloom rules over the cape. The murmur of the crowd strengthens and blends with the murmur of the sea.)

1906

CONTEXT OF *THE KING ON THE SQUARE*

HER COMING

I

WORKERS ON THE ROAD

Fringed with the flying foam,
The pier breathes both day and night.
Our slow labor, charmed
By a siren, is hard.
Under us the ocean drones.
In the port, lights flicker.
Beacons are searching keenly
For the ships beyond the breakers.
And in the sea sways the gloom –
Like scared dawns,
These subtle beams
That are stealing in the night.
Broad – the nights' embraces,
Grave – the sighs of darkness.
All of us are close, and all of us are brothers!
Long after midnight –
In the distance of an unknown land –
We accompanied
Blue ships sadly.
And the outlines of the black
Stacks and the thin spars were strange.
And the unfamiliar beasts
Had dark names.
"Bird of Foam" rode southward,
Gave a sign, having turned back:
Through the tempest, through the blizzard,
They had made out a red flag . . .
What secret did we guard?
And whose riches did we watch?
Did they sail gold bars
In to our dark coolies?
Did a wondrous bird in a cage
Bring together our shoulders?
Or did the black queen
In it timidly stand still? . . .
And as in a tale, the people are in the sea:

Each is proud of his grave burden.
Echoing the mist's songs,
The morose port thunders.

II

THIS IS HOW IT WAS

Life was yearning.
Death was cause
Of the endless blessings
Not attained here in this world.

The sky closed
Over the sea's plain
At the hour the first
Light flag appeared.

Night concealed
From insomniac orbs
Everything that occurred
Beyond the pale of the seas.

Only at sunset
In the slanting evening glow
Did reflections,
shadows
Of the ships rush on.

But not everyone had read
Sunset signs.
And the evening glow had died –
Face to moon –

The pale planet,
Rending gloom,
Knew about the coming
Hopeless depths.

III

THE SAILORS' SONG

The sea gave us
A wedding ring.
The sea kissed us
On our suntanned faces.
The sea fathoms
Became engaged!
The sea rapids
Have no fiancée.
with her, life's at liberty.
With her, death's not fearful.
She, my little mother, is cold, free.
With her, we go walking
In free, open spaces!
The blue sea!
The red sunsets!
Salt wind,
Bear our voices!
You, free wind,
Fill our sails!

IV

VOICE IN THE CLOUDS

In a hurry the sea bore us toward savage land,
To miserable shelter, and toward short sleep.
The wind stiffened. Above the sea, it resounded.
It made you feel anxious to look in the depths.

We were envious, we, the sick and the weary,
That somewhere a storm was revelling out in the seas,
And the night, without any shame, looked, like a whore,
At our dark faces, into our sick eyes.

We fought with the storm, and then squinting,
We could barely make out the way in the gloom . . .
Like an ambassador sent by the storm that was mounting,
The voice of a prophet struck the throng.

An instantaneous zigzag on stony, steep slope,
A ceremonial profile splashed in our eyes,
And in the clear rent of a cloud that was startled,
The storm started singing a merry air:

"Sad people, people so weary,
Awaken, and know joy is near!
There, where the seas start to sing of a miracle,
There wends the light of the beacon!

It is roaming, it seeks joyous findings
And watches the breakers with vigilant beam
And every moment awaits the arrival
Of large ships from a distant land!

Look how the bands of light widen,
How joyous the rush of the bubbling foam!
How triumphant the sea is! You hear – somewhere –
Beyond night and the storm, the sirens' summons!"

It seemed that its clothes were swept upwards.
A hand overshadowed the thundering distance . . .
And we awoke for new hope.
We knew: Joy, unexpected, was near! . . .

But there – the horizon aroused summer lightning,
As if in the distance, cities were burning.
And all through the night, the trains flew, just like crimson
Birds, hissing and whistling, towards the port.

The ocean was droning. The sea foam was hurling
Itself on the lighthouses' pylons like rags.
Like a drawn-out entreaty, the sirens were howling:
There the storm had overtaken the fishermen's crafts.

V

THE SHIPS ARE COMING

O, light-bearing stalks of the sea, you beacons!
    Your searchlight's a flower!
Your soil's the creation of agitation,
    Scythes of the sands.

Your stalks, O, thou ocean blossom, are hardy,
Their electrical current is powerful!
　　Your beams promise salvation
There, where sailors are perishing.

Morning will say: Take a look: You are weary with work.
　　You will find in the breakers
　　A powerless corpse
Not saved by your worry,

With a laughter that cools in blue corners
　　Of twitching lips ...
The one who escaped from your light-bearing rays.
The one who transgressed the last threshold ...

　　Invisible to eyes,
　　Under cover of night,
A conciliatory Fate will inscribe on his brow:
　　"No one's."

On us you take vengeance, electrical light!
You're not light from the dawn, you're a dream from dry land,
But with your beam, you pierce the anarchic
　　Ocean's deception on fog-laden days.

There's no comrade for us more reliable:
We lead ships through a blizzard of winter.
We are carrying overseas secrets.
Under the yoke of nocturnal haze ...

The holds are filled up with treasure!
The burdened ships hurry!
Let our star – electricity guard
Them from underwater horrors!

Across the storm, through the blizzard – ahead!
The electrical light will not die!

VI

THE SHIPS HAVE COME

Mirror-like, the ocean slumbered.
Vicious storms have all departed.
At the crystal hour of sunset,
Ships have come in sight.

They were coming, folktale fairies.
Pennants made the distance heady.
Heavily sagged their spars,
Anchors at the ready.

To the crimson evening glow, they sang a hymn.
The distance laughed, all on fire.
It was sad to part
With the deep blue farewell sea.

There already – behind that scythe or braid[23] –
Unexpectedly radiant,
In fog-enshrouded splendor,
A great beauty awaited them . . .

Then – dry land, O, passion's children,
Children of the storm – she's there for you!
Heavily fell the rigging.
A rocket bore the news.

VII

DAYLIGHT

A rocket was quietly scattering up in the sky.
The west was extinguished; the land sighed.
They stood on the road and awaited daylight,
Giving the night of return to their dream.

Lights of gray morning approach. In dawn's somnolence,

---

23 Here, as in *A Puppet Show*, Blok plays on the two meanings of the word "kosa", a braid or a scythe. In this instance, I have incorporated both meanings into the poem as separate lexical items.

There is something immeasurably sad.
There – in the ocean – in the terrestrial reservoir –
The skittish news wanders and splashes . . .

White, as white bird, in the distance
Measures the heights and the depths, and then suddenly,
With the first arrow that flies from the east,
A somnolent sound wakes up in the seas.

Over the sea, death or life is hanging.
News of victory lies in the flight of the arrow.
And we mortals don't argue the sun.
We know, it is time for our praise to be readied, prepared.

Whoever failed to wake up at first radiance
Remembers through the gloom that the hymn can't be heard
    anymore,
Senses through sleep that he's lost the experience
Of early and light and wise origins.

News of daylight from the ships,
That had tested the bad weather, reached dry land:
Turbulent crowds, in foreboding of happiness
Went to the shore to welcome the ships.

Someone tosses a garland of flowers.
Boats rush from the land that is motley.
Strong youths sit at the oars.
Modest girls take the rudders.

They sail and they sing, and the sea gets sloshed . . .
******

16 December 1904

OF LOVE, POETRY, AND GOVERNMENT SERVICE

A Dialogue

Participants in the Dialogue

A love-struck POET
A FOOL – a man of common sense and unknown rank
A COURTIER
Several BEGGARS

(Setting: A city square on a seashore. The Fool sits over the water with a fishing pole. Lost in thought, the Poet approaches him.)

> POET. More than once I've noticed you angling for fish in the waters around here. By all appearances, you're a poor fisherman?
> FOOL. I can answer your Hamletesque[24] question: Yes, my good sir. The catch is especially successful on days like today: The sea is roily, there's a column of dust. The catch goes blind and throws itself right on the hook.
> POET. So does that mean the catch is good sometimes?
> FOOL. It depends. Not too long ago I landed a huge fish. I'm sure that it's satisfied with me.
> POET. The fish is satisfied with you?
> FOOL. What's so surprising about that? I've been teaching it common sense and political economy for a long time now. But sometimes a fish is all rabid: It's so insolent, it won't swallow the hook for anything.
> POET. I don't understand your words. You talk about fish as if they were people.
> FOOL. Oh, yes, sir. A certain predilection for allegory is characteristic of such a joker and kind soul as myself: According to the testament of the Scriptures, I fish for men.
> POET. You know, it's fun to talk with you. What do you do with your fish?
> FOOL. I set them free well-trained: They're not sad anymore, they don't grumble, they don't worry about trifles. They are satisfied with things as they are, and they're ready to work.
> POET. Your words breathe ardent conviction. Oh, if only I could

---

24 An apparent allusion to Hamlet's talk with the gravedigger.

learn your science. But I'm afraid you're getting carried away: The sea is vast, and no matter what, you can't teach all the fish from scratch again.

FOOL Oh, no, I believe in them all. My science is an infectious, gay science.[25]

POET. (*Aside*.) Well now, he's read Nietzsche!

FOOL. One fish will teach another. And I myself will be free to go where I want on the light boat of common sense.

POET. Your *joie de vivre* makes me wonder ...

FOOL. (*Ecstatically.*) Oh, yes, I'm an optimist. I boldly put my hand on my heart and tell you even more: I am an idealist. I'm a patriot. I participate in making culture. Anyone who follows me will enjoy equality, satisfaction, and health, for on my banner is inscribed: Common Sense. Progress and I are one.

POET. Won't you share your experience with me?

FOOL. I'd love to, sir. I gladly cast my line to talk with you.

POET. But who are you? In order to trust you, I must know you better.

FOOL. Modestly ignoring the fact that I am the most necessary person in the city, I can introduce myself allegorically: I am the most prudent of the participants in our dialogue and thus feel a responsibility before the reader. If you prolong our conversation with idle hesitations, our readers' anger will fall on me: You're the *jeune premier* who always comes out of the water dry. I'm a simple parasite, and I value my time and my backside.

POET. (*Deep in thought*.) This guy speaks none too simply. His coarse folk wisdom soothes my sorrowing soul.

FOOL. Make up your mind as quickly as possible, sir. Your thoughts make for boring reading.

POET. You're right, friend. Health wafts from your words. But why do you keep talking about readers?

FOOL. Sir, I'm simply saying that it's time to abandon superfluous conversations and cross over to the deed itself. According to several indications, I see that the writer of our dialogue is a big-time dunder head himself! Without me, the deed won't get done. – Common sense will always come to the aid of authorial fantasy.

POET. That's it. I don't understand a thing. But I know the roots of folk wisdom are dark and full of knots. You encourage my trust. Be entrusted to my soul. Do you know who I am?

---

25 An allusion to *The Gay Science* [*Die Fröhliche Wissenschaft*] (1882) by Friedrich Nietzsche (1844–90).

FOOL. I know perfectly well. You are a poet who is melancholy amidst the vulgarity around you. You pour out your complaints in verse, which, although beautiful, is also incomprehensible, since your spirit, in all likelihood, belongs to other generations.

POET. It's true! I swear it!

FOOL. What's more, you are still a beautiful youth passionately enamored of the no less Beautiful Lady.

POET. Say no more! You are a heart-sayer! First and foremost, tell me how to behave with the Beautiful Lady.

FOOL. I advise you, first and foremost, to dedicate one of your poems to her. Or better yet – a whole volume!

POET. I did that long ago.

FOOL. In that case, you must spend hours with her above the sea, hinting that your love is no less voluminous.

POET. (*Half unconsciously.*)
In our love, wide as the sea,
That earthly shores cannot contain . . .

FOOL. Or, finally, in front of her, push away the people on the square, even if you subject yourself to recriminations for not knowing how to behave out on the streets.

POET. All these means have been tested, dear friend.

FOOL. And still, your lady remains unyielding?

POET. Alas, she does. She looks at me, but it's as if she looks through me. Her gaze is always directed afar.

FOOL. Judging by what you say, sir, your lady is very eccentric. She doesn't suffer from an inclination towards liberalism, does she?

POET. I believe that she's above all passing formulas. But freedom is dear to her – Isn't that the way you wanted to express it?

FOOL. Excuse me for expressing myself crudely: Serving those near to you makes you crude in words, though tender in soul. And so, my last bit advice to you is to write civic verse.

POET. You're right, I'll write civic verse! Accusatory verse!

FOOL. But, only once, my good sir, only once! In general I wouldn't advise you to descend into accusatory literature. That's not your domain. You're a pure artist. Your misty images will always be for a few dozen sensitive connoisseurs. Would it really be more pleasant for you to appeal to the lowest instincts of the crowd, rather than to delight the taste of the chosen?

POET. From the spirit of your wisdom I divine a profound thought: Literature must be socially oriented! It is vain to rebuke the crowd for its inattention to refined poetry! The crowd, in its own way, is sensitive, and knows what it needs! Literature must be our daily bread!

FOOL. You are still interpreting my words incorrectly. In vain you try to tear profound truths out of my soul – together with the cockleburs! Disdain for the crowd is the distinction of a lofty mind. The crowd isn't sensitive, but it has a weakness for what's pleasant; and thus social literature is harmful to it. Literature develops imagination. Imagination is the mother of the abyss. Loafers and unbalanced heads are harmful to the welfare of the people, as Gorky's heroes suffice to show. Yes, literature is positively harmful. And I'm only participating in this conversation so that it will end more quickly.

POET. What wit! You are a symbolist! I myself am no admirer of Gorky...

FOOL. So that's what "Man of letters" means! You were so enraptured by my speech that it's as if you had forgotten about your lady altogether. By the way, my main goal is to assist you in attaining her hand as quickly as possible.

POET. But I'm not in the least trying to attain her hand.... I love her with an unearthly love....

FOOL. Oh, sir, how much time we've lost to no good purpose! After all, I can only give you advice about real matters, when they involve marriage, protection, the conclusion of commercial transactions....

POET. I forgive your coarseness. It is atoned for by the depth and wisdom of your words. Do what you want, just cure me of my melancholy!

FOOL. There's nothing for you to be melancholy about. You'd better find yourself some kind of something to do. The main thing is – don't talk so slowly and pensively. It's better to be silent for a while. I notice that beggars are gathering around us: I say they'll soon disperse them. We'll enjoy the noble spectacle of order being restored.

(Enter the Courtier, who has come out for a walk. Several beggars surround him. Seeing that he can't leave, no matter what, he addresses them.)

COURTIER. Gentlemen, I'm prepared to impart to you useful instructions. Standing on guard of the interests of the country, we, the courtiers, pay careful attention to the voice of the people. I beseech you to set forth your thoughts as succinctly and as precisely as possible.

BEGGAR. I'm starving.

COURTIER. Hmm. That's succinct, but imprecise.

FOOL. Allow me to direct the attention of your Highness to the backwardness of this man. He will express himself coarsely until education touches him.

COURTIER. All of the government's forces are directed towards enlightenment. But don't worry – In our time it has become necessary to hear even more insulting things. Allow me to inquire, with whom am I speaking?

FOOL. At present, I am a servant of your Highness and a tribune of the people.

COURTIER. How pleasant to hear it. I have always waited for the appearance of people, who would dispel the misunderstanding between the people and the government. In my opinion, for this, one has only to possess common sense.

FOOL. I have served common sense my whole life, and I have eliminated any obstacle that hinders the rapprochement of both private persons and social powers.

COURTIER. In that case, as a test, I ask you to tell the people what is needed in the present case.

FOOL. (*Addressing the Beggars.*) Gentlemen, your requests, I hope, are entirely lawful. In particular, this man's wish will be considered in the near future. No less than you, the government, without a doubt, cares about the satiety of the people. But, as interested parties, you yourselves can judge that time is needed for this. At the present moment, the government is occupied with affairs that cannot be put off.

(*The Beggars are unable to object to anything. The Courtier warmly presses the Fool's hand. The Poet draws the Fool off to the side.*)

POET. Does common sense really order you to act that way?

FOOL. Yes, we acted in full accord with its dictates.

POET. Is it really impossible to feed these beggars?

FOOL. Your straightforwardness surprises me. Can you really not see that we're doing everything we can?

POET. You're putting the matter off.

FOOL. You still don't understand the gist of the matter. How old-fashioned you are! Common sense is good when it agrees with the demands of political economy.

POET. No science forces people to starve!

FOOL. Except for the most refined science. I make bold to reproach you for your lack of acquaintance with the status of this matter: If you feed one beggar, ten more will show up. If you grant indulgence to some, you put others at risk. This is higher than all personal strivings.

POET. This is an abomination, not common sense.

FOOL. Noble indignation can even advance a person. Just use it sparingly. Then anyone will see that you're bringing your personal interests to the altar of community.

COURTIER. (*Surrounded by Beggars, makes a speech.*) I guarantee, gentlemen, that all of you, one way or another, will be satisfied. The slogan of the government of a free country is the basis of a solid legality. This basis is already in and of itself fruitful. (*His voice becomes sincere.*) From it, as from a seed of grain, a magnificent harvest comes. What serves as the basis of the modern state is no longer the dark tyranny of rulers, but the well-founded labor and humanitarian relationship between subjects and the government.

POET. (*To the Fool.*) I'm amazed at the patience of this windbag.

FOOL. I swear there is absolutely nothing to be amazed at. These dialogues between beggars and courtiers have been repeated a hundred times before. The author of the dialogue, which I have wormed my way into, will apparently tread along a beaten path. It's to his advantage to represent any courtier in a ridiculous light.

POET. Again you speak in symbols. Is it really possible to forget that there exist rich and poor?

FOOL. Allow me to point out to you that it is unbecoming a poet to utter banalities and sentimentalities. Common sense would help you to be above all these petty interests you have become so engrossed in. It's no wonder that your melancholy has you so confused.

POET. I understand you're teaching me folk wisdom. But what if I'm unable to endure eternal tragedy? What if I smash my head on what you call banality and sentimentality?

FOOL. Your ideas are profoundly modern. They have been inherited by our century from the nineteenth. But remember that Fyodor Mikhailovich Dostoevsky, the bard of the insulted and the injured, was also an admirer of autocracy, – and you will understand me.

POET. Nonetheless, I will write accusatory verse . . .

FOOL. Again! You drive me crazy! Spare me, no more shall I give you advice. I suggest you appeal to the Courtier and try to better your career.

(The Poet proudly, but obediently, makes his way towards the Courtier. The Courtier looks graciously at the Poet.)

COURTIER. It seems, you have come to me with some affair or another, young man. Judging by your dress and manners, I suspect that you belong to good society and possess an upbringing sufficiently subtle so as not to impede men of practical affairs with ticklish requests. If I'm not mistaken, you're a poet?

POET. (*Somewhat flattered.*) Yes, until this very day, I wrote poems, but I never expected them to be known abroad. As such, your acquaintance with them is all the more unexpected for me.

COURTIER. I know your poems well, young man. You will find in me a veritable connoisseur of the subjective lyric. If I am not mistaken, you, much as Petrarch once, created in your mystic quests an intimate cult of woman and womanly love?

POET. That is not it exactly.... But, of course, ...

COURTIER. Oh, forgive me, if I haven't understood you fully. Constant governmental worries, you know, make a person less sensitive to the sublime. But in recompense, the consciousness of a sacredly fulfilled duty is the reward for a certain loss of personality. For a busy man, there cannot be too much hesitating or regretting.

POET. Your last words are very important to me. It was precisely the desire to sacrifice my imagination for the social good that brought me to you.

COURTIER. Oh, how I love youth! You are all in these extremes! At your age, I too had just such a hot head, young man. Frankly, I too once wrote verse...

POET. Oh, really?

COURTIER. (*Interrupting severely.*) ... But it seemed to me that the poetic imagination would be a hindrance to my calling. And now, having given myself over forever to the welfare of others, and having lost my personal life (as you see, they don't even let me go for a walk in peace), I sometimes regret that I ceased to write verse.... Perhaps, the poet in me has perished. (*Blows his nose.*) And so, quoting from my personal experience, I hasten to forewarn you that to bury talent is a sin.

POET. I agree.

COURTIER. The subjective lyric is a grand affair, young man. It gives the elect hours of æsthetic leisure and allows them, if but for a minute, to forget the voice of the capricious rabble. Oh, I am ready to wish that all literature were akin to your poems! Such poetry does not corrupt morals. After all, nothing is accessible for the uninitiated, except for their unbridled desires: To eat, to have a roof overhead – that's all they need, as you yourself may now be satisfied. To make up for it, the chosen, wiping their sweaty brow, may touch the unpolluted brim of a sacred chalice with their lips. (*Extraordinarily satisfied with his speech.*)

POET. I'm flattered by your attention to the Muses. Your words have inspired me. All the more so, since meeting such a well-rounded man as you, I would like to avail myself of your instruction. I consider it my duty to answer your frankness with frankness: Lengthy service to the Muses begets melancholy. Beneath my feet yawn abysses. Double visions visit me. I want a firm will, pure desire, but I am not fit for life. In women, tenderness and mendacity attract me and repulse me alike. I seek one who will cast living seeds into my soul, which has been torn up, but which is ready for sowing.

COURTIER. Your confession seizes me by the heart. Especially noteworthy is what you said about women. It is both witty and profound. How familiar this is to me. To love one, but to be incapable of preferring her to another . . . (*With a smile, he recollects something.*)

POET. That's not exactly what I said. I wanted to say that not about two, but about one.

COURTIER. In that case, this is all the more witty and subtle, young man! Your eloquence is a rare trait in people of our century.

POET. (*Grows sad.*)

COURTIER. Now there are so few really useful and necessary people that I have, in earnest, designs on you. Don't you have some special request for me?

POET. It seems to me sometimes that I could rid myself of my melancholy in government service.

COURTIER. That is just what I wanted to hear from you, young man! There is no reason for me to object – We are in complete solidarity in our sympathies and tastes. I hope you won't refuse to accept my offers. Your speech about duplicity created a brilliant combination in my mind: We will prepare you for a diplomatic career.

FOOL. (*Congratulates the Poet, who is still sad.*)

COURTIER. (*To the Fool.*) You too have rendered me inestimable services. An assignment in my administration will be found for you as well. (*Secretly points at the Beggars, who are still standing not far off.*)

FOOL. (*Signals that he has understood.*)

COURTIER. (*Addressing the Beggars.*) Gentlemen, we have considered your requests. I am happy to say to you that today the people have not disappointed the hopes of their government. Having mingled closely with you, I have discovered two suitable servants for the government. This clearly bears witness to the fact that the strengths of the people have not weakened. Nor shall our care for you grow weak. (*Quickly leaves.*)

FOOL. (*To the Poet.*) And so, my judicious intervention has brought you benefit. Long live patriotic poetry and government service! And, most important, long live the common sense that reconciles them!

(*Runs after the Poet, who is moving off. After a little while, a desperate brawl can be heard behind the stage. The Fool, all dishevelled, runs out.*)

FOOL. How's that for poetic temperament? He tore out a clump of my hair and started screaming that he didn't want to be a diplomat! My efforts to intercede for him were all for naught! Look how I've suffered for the truth, and listen to my noble moral: No one, ever, anywhere . . .

(Without finishing what he is saying, he rushes to find his fishing pole, since new victims of common sense are approaching . . .)

1906

THE UNKNOWN WOMAN

A woman of truly unusual beauty was depicted in the portrait. She had been photographed in a black silk dress of extraordinarily simple and elegant design. Her hair, apparently dark red, was done up simply as she might have worn it around the house. Her eyes were dark, deep, and her forehead was pensive. The expression of her face was passionate and seemed somehow haughty. She was somewhat thin in the face, perhaps, and pale...

Dostoevsky, The Idiot

"And how did you know that it was me? Where did you see me before? What is this really, is it as if I had seen you somewhere?

"Is it as if I had also seen you somewhere?"

"Where? Where?"

"It's exactly as if I had seen your eyes somewhere... Yet that couldn't be! It is I who so... I have never been here. Perhaps in a dream..."

Dostoevsky, The Idiot

Dramatis Personae

THE UNKNOWN WOMAN
THE BLUE ONE
THE ASTRONOMER
THE POET
VISITORS to a bar and a drawing room
Two DOORMEN[26]

---

26 Blok omits from the dramatis personae a Gentleman, who plays a small, but significant role in the second "vision," as well as the patrons of the bar in the first vision and the party-goers of vision three.

FIRST VISION

(A little neighborhood bar on the street. The dull white light of an acetylene lamp gutters in its crumpled shade. Absolutely identical ships with huge flags are depicted on the wallpaper. With their bows, they cut through the deep blue waters. Beyond the door, which often opens, letting patrons in, and beyond the big windows, which are decorated with ivy, passersby in fur coats and girls in kerchiefs walk by under a blue evening snow. Behind the counter, on which has been hoisted a cask with a gnome and the inscription "Mug and Goblet," are two men who are utterly alike one another: Both with parts and hair that stands up, both in green aprons, only the Owner has a mustache that droops, while his brother, the Waiter, has a mustache that stands up. A drunken old man – the very image of Verlaine – sits by one window at a little table. By another sits a pale man without a mustache, the very likeness of Hauptmann.

Several drunken groups.)

Conversation in one group

 ONE. I bought this hat for twenty-five rubles. But for you Sasha, I wouldn't think of letting you have it for less than thirty.
 OTHER. (*Convincingly and taking offense.*) Yeah, you're lying! . . . Why don't you come over here . . . I'll . . .
 THIRD. (*Mustachioed. Yells.*) Shut up! Stop your fighting! Another bottle, my man.

(The Waiter runs up. The beer gurgles. Silence. A lone patron gets up in the corner and goes to the counter with an unsteady gait. He starts rummaging around in the shiny serving bowl with boiled crayfish.)

 OWNER. If I may, sir. That isn't allowed. You'll pick over all of our crayfish with your hands. Nobody will eat them then.

(The patron, mumbling, walks away.)

Conversation in another group

 SEMINARIAN. And she danced, I tell you, my dear friend, like something made in heaven. I could just take her by her little white hands and kiss her, I tell you, right on her little lips . . .

DRINKING BUDDY. (*Laughs shrilly.*) Ho, ho, Vasya here is off in la-la land. He turned as crimson as a poppy! And what sort of love is she for you? What sort of love? ... Huh? ...

(*Everyone laughs shrilly.*)

SEMINARIAN. (*Completely red.*) And I say, my dear friend, it's not good to laugh. So I would take her like that and carry her away from immodest gazes, and on the street she'd dance in front of me in the white snow ... as a bird would fly. And suddenly I would have wings – and I would fly up after her over the white snows ...

(*Everyone guffaws.*)

SECOND DRINKING BUDDY. Watch out, Vasya, better look out that you don't fly too much over the first snow ...
FIRST DRINKING BUDDY. You'd be better off flying over the frost, or you and your sweetheart might fall right in the dirt ...
SECOND DRINKING BUDDY. Dreamer.
SEMINARIAN. (*He becomes completely dreamy.*) Oh, dear pals-o-mine, not having studied in the seminary, I tell you, you don't understand tender feelings. So what do you say, how about some more beer ...
VERLAINE. (*Mumbles loudly to himself.*) To each his own. To each his own ...

(*Hauptmann makes expressive signals to the Waiter. Enter a Redheaded Man and a Girl in a kerchief.*)

GIRL. (*To the Waiter.*) A bottle of stout, Misha. (*Continues telling a story quickly to the Man.*) ... only she, my dear, went out, when suddenly she realized she'd forgotten to treat the lady of the house to a beer. So now she goes back, and sure enough he's got the chest opened up, and he's digging around in it. He's digging around in it and tossing things everywhere. He didn't think she'd be back so soon ... So anyway, honey, she starts screaming, and he tries to shut her up. So then the landlady runs in, and she starts screaming, and starts yelling for the doorman. So you know what, honey? They take the guy right down to the police station ... (*Suddenly interrupts herself.*) Give me twenty kopecks.

(*The Man glumly digs out twenty kopecks.*)

GIRL. You sad about something?
MAN. Drink and shut up.

(They are silent. They drink. A Young Man runs in and happily rushes over to Hauptmann.)

YOUNG MAN. Kostya, my friend, she is waiting at the door! . . .
HAUPTMANN. So what? Let her wait. Let's drink.
VERLAINE. *(Mumbles loudly.)* And to all people – their own pursuit . . . And to each – his own concern.

(In comes the Poet. Calls the Waiter over.)

POET. Can I buy you a round?
WAITER. *(A born humorist.)* It would be a great honor, sir . . . From such a renowned personage, sir . . .

(Runs out for the beer. The Poet takes out his notebook. Silence. The acetylene hisses. Pretzels crunch.

The Waiter brings the Poet a bottle of beer and sits down on the edge of the chair across from him.)

POET. Just listen to this. You wander through the streets, catching snippets of unknown words. Then – you come here and bear your soul to some dummy.
WAITER. Incomprehensible, sir, but highly refined, sir . . .

(Tears himself from the stool and runs at the call of a patron. The Poet writes in his notebook.)

GIRL. *(Hums.)*
   How I do love her . . .
   And she, for love . . .

(Waiter returns to the Poet.)

POET. *(Drinks.)* You see a lot of women's faces. Hundreds of eyes, big and deep, blue, dark, light. Narrow ones, like the eyes of a lynx. Wide open ones, like a baby's. You love them. You desire them. There cannot be a man, who doesn't love them. You have to love them.
WAITER. At your service, sir.
POET. And in the midst of the fire of their gazes, in the midst of the

whirlwind of their gazes, one face suddenly arises, as if blossoming under the blue snow: The singularly sublime visage of the Unknown Woman under a thick, dark veil... There the plumes wave on her head... There her narrow hand bound by a glove holds her rustling dress: There, she passes by slowly... She passes by...

(Drinks greedily.)

>VERLAINE. *(Mumbles.)* And everything passes by. And to everyone – his own worry.
>SEMINARIAN. *(With slurred speech.)* She danced like a heavenly angel, I tell you. You devils and thieves aren't worth her little finger. But who cares? Let's drink.
>DRINKING BUDDY. Dreamer. And that's why you drink. All of us are dreamers. Gimme a kiss, buddy.

(They embrace.)

>SEMINARIAN. No one could love her like I could. We'll live out our sad life on the white snow. She'll dance, and I'll play the accordion. And we'll fly. And we'll fly up to the silvery moon itself. God damn you, I'm telling you, dear buddies, don't go poking your dirty, idiot noses there. But still, I love you very much and hold you in high esteem. If you don't drink from the same bottle, you don't know friendship.

(All guffaw.)

>DRINKING BUDDY. Oho, Vasya! Well put! Gimme a kiss, buddy!
>YOUNG MAN. *(To Hauptmann.)* However it will be. How long is she supposed to wait out in the frost? She'll be completely frozen. Brother, let's go, Kostya.
>HAUPTMANN. Drop it. If you indulge the female temper, then nothing will remain of a man – but to spit in his ugly mug. Let her cool her heels, and let us sit here for a bit yet.

(The Young Man obeys. All the patrons drink and get tipsy. A Man in a tattered yellow coat, who's been sitting by himself, gets up and addresses a speech to the whole bar.)

>MAN IN THE COAT. My dear sirs! I have a little something here – a highly valuable miniature. *(Pulls out of his pocket a cameo.)* There it is, sirs, if you please: On one side, the depiction of an emblem, on the other, a pleasant lady in a tunic sitting on a globe

and holding a scepter over the globe: Submit, she says, obey – and nothing more!

(*Everyone laughs approvingly. Some come up and look the cameo over.*)

POET. (*Inebriated.*) The eternal tale. This is – She – the Ruler of the World. She holds a staff and rules the world. All of us are enchanted by Her.
MAN IN THE COAT. I'm glad to serve the Russian intelligentsia. I'll sell it cheap, though it wasn't cheap. But, as they say, anything for a friend. I can see that you're a connoisseur. You can tell by your hands.

(*The Poet gives him a coin. He takes the cameo, looks it over. The Man in the Coat sits down in his seat. A conversation continues just between two who are sitting at a separate little table.*)

FIRST MAN. (*Picks up a humor magazine.*) And now the time has come for us to have some fun. So listen, Vanya (*Solemnly unfolds the magazine and reads.*): "Loving spouses. The husband, 'Dear, go to mama today and ask her to . . .'"

(*Beforehand starts guffawing desperately.*)

SECOND MAN. How do you like that, damn it, that's good!
FIRST MAN. (*Continues reading.*) "And ask her to . . . give little Katya a little doll . . ."

(*Guffaws frightfully hard.*)

FIRST MAN. (*Reads.*) "The Wife says, 'What do you mean, dear? Little Katya is already twenty years old. (*He can hardly finish reading from laughter.*) The time has come to give her a little groom, not a little doll'."

(*Thunderous guffaws.*)

SECOND MAN. Now that's a good one!
FIRST MAN. That's what's called giving him what's for!
SECOND MAN. Can't deny it, they got a way with words! . . .

(*And again the lone patron rummages through the serving bowl. He pulls the crayfish out by the claws. He holds them up and puts them back. Again the Owner chases him off.*)

> POET. (*Looks the cameo over.*) The eternal return. She will envelop the globe. And again we will be subject to Her enchantment. There She whirls her flourishing staff . . . And I whirl with Her . . . Under the blue . . . under the evening snow . . .
> SEMINARIAN. She dances . . . Dances . . . I'm on the accordion, and she dances to the accordion . . . (*Makes drunken gestures, as if catching at something.*) There, missed . . . missed again . . . But you devils couldn't catch her either, if I couldn't catch her . . .

(*The walls of the little bar slowly, slowly start to spin. The ceiling tilts; one end of it stretches out infinitely upward. The ships on the wallpaper, it seems, sail close up, but still can't sail all the way in. The Man in the Coat, who has already sat down next to somebody, yells through the confused general chatter.*)

> MAN IN THE COAT. No, sir, I'm a connoisseur. I love sharp cheese, you know, the round kind, like this. (*Makes circular gestures.*) I forget the name.
> HIS INTERLOCUTOR. (*Uncertainly.*) Have you . . . tried it?
> MAN IN THE COAT. What, tried it? You think I didn't? I've eaten Rochefort!
> INTERLOCUTOR. (*Under whom a stool shakes.*) You know . . . Luxembourg . . . smells so bad . . . and it wiggles, it wiggles . . .

(*Smacks his lips and moves his fingers.*)

> MAN IN THE COAT. (*Gets up with inspiration.*) Swiss! . . . Now there's something, sir!

(*Snaps his fingers.*)

> INTERLOCUTOR. (*Winks and expresses doubt.*) You can't impress me with that . . .
> MAN IN THE COAT. (*Loudly, like the discharge of a rifle.*) Brie!
> INTERLOCUTOR. Now that's . . . that's . . . you know . . .
> MAN IN THE COAT. (*Threateningly.*) Do you know what?
> INTERLOCUTOR (*Crushed.*) In terms of price . . .

(*Everything turns round, it seems, and turns over. The ships on the wallpaper sail, churning the blue water up into foam. For a minute, it seems that everything stands upside down.*)

> VERLAINE. (*Mumbles.*) To everything its turn . . . And to all, a time to go home . . .

HAUPTMANN. (*Shouts.*) She's a bitch, so just let her cool her heels. And we're going to drink!
GIRL. (*Sings in the Man's ear.*) Farewell, man of my desires . . .
SEMINARIAN. The snow dances. And we dance too. The accordion is crying. And I'm crying too. All of us are crying.
POET. Sky-blue snow. It whirls. It falls softly. Sky-blue orbs. A thick veil. She passes by slowly. The heavens open. Appear! Appear!

(*The whole bar seems to have dived somewhere. The walls part. The ceiling, having tilted once and for all, opens the sky – wintry, blue, cold. In the deep blue evening snows opens:*)

5. Lentulov's sketch for the Redheaded Gentleman from *The Unknown Woman*, Moscow 1918
Courtesy of Union of Theater Workers' Library, Moscow

THE SECOND VISION

(The same evening. The end of a street at the edge of the city. The last houses, breaking off suddenly, reveal a wide perspective: A dark, empty bridge across a big river. Quiet boats with signal lights slumber along both sides of the bridge. An avenue, endless, straight as an arrow, and framed by rows of streetlights and trees that are white from hoarfrost, stretches beyond the bridge. In the air, the snow flutters down and turns starry.)

    ASTRONOMER. *(On the bridge.)*
        The star-filled night is light.
        A look has just two wings.
        But it's impossible to count the stars –
        The Milky Way is misty
        And my poor sight grows dim . . .
        Who is this drunk?

(Two bouncers drag the drunken Poet under the arms.)

    INFURIATED DOORMEN.
        He's a patron of that little inn.
        We'll make short work of him!
        Hey, Vanya, tweak his nose!
        Hey, Vasya, give him a jolt!

(They drag the Poet further.)

    ASTRONOMER.
        A new star is rising.
        It is more dazzling than the rest.
        The darkish water is motionless.
        And in it, the star's reflected.
        Oh, it's falling, flying, the star . . .
        Fly here! Here! Here!

(Describing a slow arc, a bright and heavy star slides across the sky. A moment later, a beautiful woman in black, with a surprised look in her widely opened eyes, walks across the bridge. Everything becomes as in a folktale – the dark bridge and the slumbering, blue boats. The Unknown Woman, still keeping her pale, falling brilliance, grows cold by the railings of the bridge. The snow, eternally youthful, dresses her shoulders and powders her figure. She, like a statue, waits.

One just as Blue as she walks up on the bridge from the dark avenue. He is also covered by snow. He is also beautiful. He undulates slightly, like a tranquil blue flame.)

BLUE ONE.
   In the brilliance of this waning winter's night,
   Turn to me your face, your own,
   With snow you're softly wafting –
   Give to me your light snow.

(She turns her eyes toward him.)

UNKNOWN WOMAN.
   These orbs are stars that are dying,
   Wandering off the path.
   I pined for you on high,
   My own, who lightly wafts.

(His blue cloak is strewn with snowy stars.)

BLUE ONE.
   In your frosty blue,
   There are many stars.
   In my iron hand
   Is a bright sword.
UNKNOWN WOMAN.
   Drop from your iron hand
   Your bright sword.
   In my frosty blue
   You can't count the stars.

(The Blue One dallies in white light. A beam of it shines light on the background of his cloak, as if he were leaning on a sword.)

BLUE ONE.
   Centuries flowed by like dreams.
   I have waited so long for you on this earth.
UNKNOWN WOMAN.
   Centuries flowed by like moments
   In space. I glided as a star.
BLUE ONE.
   You glimmered from your height
   On my blue cloak.

UNKNOWN WOMAN.
    Into my eyes you looked.
    Do you often look up at the sky?
BLUE ONE.
    I can lift my eyes no more:
    My gaze is bound by you, my falling one.
UNKNOWN WOMAN.
    Can you utter earthly words to me?
    Why are you dressed all in blue?
BLUE ONE.
    I looked up at the sky too long:
    That's why my eyes and cloak are blue.
UNKNOWN WOMAN.
    Who are you?
BLUE ONE.
        A poet.
UNKNOWN WOMAN.
            Of what do you sing?
BLUE ONE.
    Only about you.
UNKNOWN WOMAN.
    Have you been waiting long?
BLUE ONE.
        Many centuries.
UNKNOWN WOMAN.
            Are you alive or dead?
BLUE ONE.
    I don't know.
UNKNOWN WOMAN.
            Are you young?
BLUE ONE.
                I'm beautiful.
UNKNOWN WOMAN.
    A falling maiden-star
    Wants earthly speech.
BLUE ONE.
    Only of mysteries do I know words.
    Mine is only the solemn kind of speech.
UNKNOWN WOMAN.
    Do you know my name?
BLUE ONE.
    I don't, and it's better not to know.

UNKNOWN WOMAN.
    Do you see my eyes?
BLUE ONE.
    I do. They're like stars.
UNKNOWN WOMAN.
    Do you see my shapely figure?
BLUE ONE.
    Yes. You're dazzling.

(Earthly passion awakens in her voice.)

UNKNOWN WOMAN.
    Do you want to take me in your arms?
BLUE ONE.
    I don't dare to touch you.
UNKNOWN WOMAN.
    You can touch my lips.

(The Blue One's cloak flickers, disappearing under the snow.)

UNKNOWN WOMAN.
    Do you know passion?
BLUE ONE. *(Softly.)*
    My blood is silent.
UNKNOWN WOMAN.
    Do you know wine?
BLUE ONE. *(Still more softly.)*
    The astral drink is sweeter than wine.
UNKNOWN WOMAN.
    Do you love me?

(The Blue One is silent.)

UNKNOWN WOMAN.
    My blood has started to heat.

(Silence.)

UNKNOWN WOMAN.
    My heart is filled with poison –
    I'm shapelier than any of your maidens.
    I'm more beautiful than your ladies.
    I'm more passionate than your brides.

(The Blue One slumbers, all strewn with snow.)

UNKNOWN WOMAN.
   How sweet you have it on earth!

(The Blue One is no longer there. A blue snow pillar spins around, and it seems that there hadn't been anyone on that spot. As if to make up for it, right next to the Unknown Woman a passing Gentleman tips his bowler.)

GENTLEMAN.
   Were you conversing with someone?
   But there's no one here.
   Your delightful voice resounded
   In the empty expanse ...
UNKNOWN WOMAN.
   Where is he?
GENTLEMAN.
   Oh, yes, doubtlessly, you
   Were waiting for someone just now!
   Allow me an immodest question ...
   Who was your invisible friend?
UNKNOWN WOMAN.
   He was beautiful. In a blue cloak.
GENTLEMAN.
   O, the romance of the female soul.
   And on the streets, do you see
   Men in blue cloaks?
   What exactly was his name?
UNKNOWN WOMAN.
   He called himself a poet.
GENTLEMAN.
   I'm a poet too! I'm a poet too!
   At the very least, looking
   Into your eyes sublime,
   I could sing a couplet for you:
   "Ooh, my, you're so fine."
UNKNOWN WOMAN.
   Do you want to love me?
GENTLEMAN.
   Oh, yes! I would be delighted.
UNKNOWN WOMAN.
   Can you take me in your arms?
GENTLEMAN.
   I'd like to know why

I can't take you in my arms?
UNKNOWN WOMAN.
    And when you touch my lips,
    Will you caress me?
GENTLEMAN.
    Let's go, my beauty!
    "Your every wish is my command,"
    As old man Shakespeare said . . .
    So you see now that I too
    Am no stranger to poetry!

(The Unknown Woman obediently gives him her hand.)

GENTLEMAN.
    What is your name?
UNKNOWN WOMAN.
      Hold on.
    Let me remember. In the sky, amongst the stars,
    I didn't have a name . . .
    But here on the blue earth,
    I like the name "Maria" . . .
    Call me "Maria."
GENTLEMAN.
    As you wish, my beauty.
    All I need to know is
    What to whisper to you tonight.

(Leads the Unknown Woman away by the hand. The blue snow covers up their trail. The Astronomer is again on the bridge. He is in anguish. Stretches his hands to the sky. Lifts his gaze.)

ASTRONOMER.
    The beautiful star isn't there anymore!
    The blue void is empty.
    I lost the rhythm
    Of my astral songs!
    From now on I'm cut off from the sound
    Of the jingling song of the luminaries!
    Today in my tower,
    With a mournful hand, I will enter
    Into my long scroll
    The news of the falling of the brightest star . . .
    And I will call it softly
    By its distant name,

By a name that comforts the ear:
"Maria" – Let that be its name.
In my yellow scroll
It will be inscribed
By my lonely hand:
"The star Maria fell.
It will no longer gaze upon my eyes.
The Astronomer remains alone."

(Cries quietly. The Poet goes up on the bridge from the avenue.)

POET.
    I adjure you by all that's holy!
    By your anguish!
    By your bride, if
    You have a bride!
    Tell me, was there
    A tall woman in black here?
ASTRONOMER.
    Crude people! Leave me alone.
    I haven't seen any woman since
    My star fell.
POET.
    I understand your grief.
    Like you, I am also alone.
    You're probably like me – a poet.
    You didn't happen to see
    An Unknown Woman in the blue snows?
ASTRONOMER.
    I don't remember. Many walk here,
    And I deeply regret
    That I didn't see yours.
POET.
    O, if you'd seen her,
    You'd forget your star.
ASTRONOMER.
    It's not for you to talk about stars.
    You are much too thoughtless.
    And I would ask you
    Not to stick your nose into my profession.
POET.
    I will suffer all of your insults!
    Believe me, I have been humiliated
    Not a bit less than you . . .

>   Oh, if I hadn't been drunk,
>   I would have followed her!
>   But those two were dragging me away
>   When I noticed her...
>   Then I fell into a snowdrift.
>   They went away cursing,
>   After they dumped me...
>   I don't remember if I slept for long...
>   When I awoke, I remembered that the snow
>   Had covered her tender trail.
> ASTRONOMER.
>   I can vaguely recall
>   Something that will make you sad:
>   It's true, they were leading you off,
>   Giving you shoves and kicks.
>   And your step was uncertain...
>   Then, I remember through my sleep
>   How a lady walked up on the bridge,
>   And a blue gentleman walked up to her.
> POET.
>   Oh, no!... The Blue gentleman...
> ASTRONOMER.
>   I don't know what they talked about.
>   I didn't look at them anymore.
>   Then they probably left...
>   I was so preoccupied with my own...
> POET.
>   And the snow covered their tracks!...
>   I won't meet Her anymore!
>   Meetings like this
>   Happen but once in a lifetime...

(Both weep beneath the blue snow.)

> ASTRONOMER.
>   Is it worth crying about that?
>   My grief is much more profound:
>   I lost the astral rhythm!
> POET.
>   I lost the rhythm of my soul.
>   I hope that's more important.
> ASTRONOMER.
>   Sorrow will enter into my scroll:
>   "The star Maria fell!"

POET.
> A beautiful name: "Maria!"
> I will write in verse:
> "Where art thou, Maria?
> The dawn I do not see."

ASTRONOMER.
> Well, your sorrow will pass!
> You need only compose
> Verses that are lengthy!
> What is there to cry about then?

POET.
> As for you, Mr. Astronomer,
> It's enough to write in your scroll
> For the good of your students:
> "The star Maria has fallen."

(Both are sad beneath the blue snow. They disappear in it. The snow is sad too. It has already powdered both the bridge and the ships. It has built white walls on the canvas of the trees, along the walls of the houses, on the telegraph wires. Both the ground and the river in the distance rise up as white walls, so that everything is white, except for the signal lights on the ships and the illuminated windows of the houses. The snowy walls thicken. They seem to be close, one after another. Little by little there opens:)

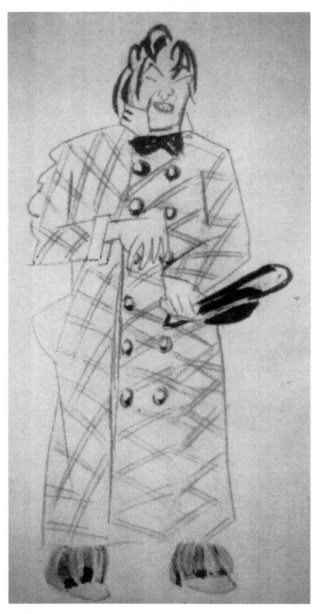

6. Lentulov's sketch for the Man in a Coat from *The Unknown Woman*, Moscow 1918
Courtesy of Union of Theater Workers' Library, Moscow

THE THIRD VISION

(A large drawing room with white walls, on which electric lamps shine brightly. The door to the anteroom is open. A delicate little ring announces the arrival of the guests. The hosts and their guests are already sitting on couches, armchairs, and wooden chairs. The Hostess is an elderly lady, stiff as a poker. In front of her is a basket of biscuits, a bowl of fruit, and a cup of steaming tea. Across from her a deaf Old Man with a senile face chews and gulps. Of the young men, all in impeccable smoking jackets, one part talks with other ladies, while the other part crowds in a herd in the corners. A general din of senseless conversations.

The Host greets the guests in the entryway, and at first yells to each in a wooden voice: "A-a-ah!," and then utters some banality.

At the present moment, he is occupied with this very thing.)

> HOST. *(In the entryway.)* A-a-ah! Well, you've really bundled yourself up, dear fellow!
> VOICE OF GUEST. It's cold to be sure, let me tell you! I have a fur hat on and still I froze.

(The Guest blows his nose. Because the conversation in the drawing room has been exhausted for some reason, you can hear the Host say to the Guest confidentially:)

> HOST. And where was it sewn?
> GUEST. At Chevalier's.

(The tails of the Host's frock coat protrude from the doorway. The Host looks the fur hat over.)

> HOST. How much did you pay?
> GUEST. A thousand.

(The Hostess, trying to change the topic, yells:)

> HOSTESS. Cher Ivan Pavlovich! Come in! You're just the person we've been waiting for! You see, Arkady Romanovich has promised to sing for us today!

(Walking up to the Hostess, Arkady Romanovich makes various gestures which are meant to show that he has a low opinion of himself.

With her own gestures, the Hostess tries to show him the opposite.)

>YOUNG MAN NAMED GEORGE. Your Serpantini is an utter fool, Misha. To dance as she did yesterday means to have no shame.
>YOUNG MAN NAMED MISHA. You, understand absolutely nothing, George! I am madly in love. Like few others could be. Imagine, she has a completely classical figure – her arms, legs ...
>GEORGE. I went there to enjoy art. I can look at legs in another place.
>HOSTESS. What's this you're going on about there, Georgy Nikolaevich? Oh, about Serpantini! A nightmare, wasn't it? In the first place, to interpret music is really only impudence. I love music so passionately that I will not allow it to be violated for any reason, for any reason. And then, to dance without a costume, that's ... that's I don't know what! I led my daughter out.
>GEORGE. I agree with you wholeheartedly. But Mikhail Ivanovich here is of a different opinion.
>HOSTESS. How can you, Mikhail Ivanovich! There can't be two opinions here! I understand that young people get carried away, but at a public concert ... when they depict Bach with their legs ... I myself am a musician ... I love music passionately ... However ...

(The Old Man, who is sitting across from the Hostess, unexpectedly and simply blurts out:)

>OLD MAN. Whore house.

(Continues slurping tea and chewing biscuits. The Hostess blushes and turns to one of the ladies.)

>MISHA. Oh, George, none of you understand anything! You think that was interpreting music? Serpantini herself is the embodiment of music. She swims on waves of sound, and it seems as if you're swimming with her yourself. Her body, its lines, its harmonious movements, aren't they just like the sounds themselves? Whoever truly feels music won't be offended for its sake. Your attitude to music is too abstract ...
>GEORGE. Dreamer! Now you've got things wound up. You build up all kinds of theories without listening to or seeing anything

else. I'm not even talking about music, and who cares in the end! I would be very happy to see all this in a room especially set aside for it. But you've got to agree, not to announce in the playbill that Serpantini will be wrapped in a simple rag – that puts everybody in an very awkward position. If I had known, I wouldn't have taken my fiancée.

(Misha absentmindedly rummages around in the basket with biscuits.)

GEORGE. Listen, leave the biscuits alone. Who wants to eat them after you've been picking through them all? Look how my cousin is looking at you. This is all because you're so absentminded. Dreamers!

(Misha, mumbling confusedly, withdraws to another corner.)

OLD MAN. *(All of a sudden to the Hostess.)* Nina! Sit still. Your dress is unbuttoned in the back.
HOSTESS. *(Blushing.)* That's enough, Uncle! Not in front of everyone! You're too ... frank ...

(Tries to button her dress without drawing attention to herself. A young Lady flits into the room. After her comes an enormous Redheaded Gentleman.)

LADY. Oh, hello, hello! Allow me to introduce you, my fiancé.
REDHEADED GENTLEMAN. Pleased to meet you.

(Sullenly withdraws to the corner.)

LADY. Please, pay him no mind. He's very shy. Oh, you won't believe what has happened! ...

(Hurriedly drinks tea and, in a whisper, relates something piquant to the Hostess, to judge by the way both of them fidget on the couch and giggle.)

LADY. *(Suddenly turns around to her fiancé.)* Do you have my handkerchief?

(The fiancé sullenly pulls out a kerchief.)

LADY. Would you really begrudge me that?
REDHEADED GENTLEMAN. Drink, and shut up.

(They are silent. They drink. A Young Man runs in and joyfully rushes over

to another young man. It is easy to recognize in the latter the one who led the Unknown Woman off.)

YOUNG MAN. Kostya, my friend, she's waiting at the d- ...

(Cuts himself off in mid-sentence. Everything becomes uncommonly strange. It's as if everyone remembered all of a sudden that somewhere the exact same words had been uttered in the exact same order. Mikhail Ivanovich casts a strange glance at the Poet, who walks in at this moment. The Poet, pale, makes a general bow on the threshold to the hushed drawing room.)

HOSTESS. *(With a strained look.)* You are just the person we've been waiting for. I hope you'll recite something for us. It's a strange evening tonight. Our peaceful conversation is faltering.
OLD MAN. *(Blurts out.)* It's like somebody died and gave up their soul to God.
HOSTESS. Oh, uncle, stop! You'll scare everyone off for good ... Good Lord! Let's talk of something new ... *(To the Poet.)* Won't you recite something for us?
POET. With pleasure ... if it would interest ...
HOSTESS. Ladies and gentlemen! Quiet! Our wonderful poet will read for us a wonderful poem. I hope it will be about the beautiful lady again [27] ...

(Everyone quiets down. The Poet takes his place by the wall, directly across from the door to the entryway, and recites:)

POET.
    The snow already ran off of the rooftiles.
    The roofs were glittering, revealing themselves
    When inside the cathedral, in the dark niche,
    Her pearls shone.
    And from the icon, in tender roses,
    She haltingly descended ...

(A shrill bell in the entryway. The Hostess imploringly clasps her hands in the direction of the Poet. He breaks off his recital. Everyone looks to the entryway with curiosity.)

---

[27] A bit of self-irony. Blok's first collection of poetry was entitled *Verses about the Beautiful Lady*. This play issues from a period when Blok had broken with the poetics of his earlier work. The play *The Unknown Woman* constitutes a rethinking of the ethereal and otherworldly Beautiful Lady.

HOST. Just a moment. I beg your pardon.

(Goes out into the entryway, where he doesn't shout: "A-a-ah!" Silence.)

VOICE OF HOST. How may I be of service?

(A woman's voice answers something. The Host appears on the threshold.)

HOST. Nina, dear, it's some lady. I can't make anything out. Probably, for you. Excuse us, ladies and gentlemen, excuse us . . .

(Smiles confusedly in all directions. The Hostess goes to the entryway and shuts the door tightly behind her. The guests whisper.)

YOUNG MAN. *(In a corner.)* It can't be . . .
ANOTHER. *(Hiding behind him.)* Yes, I assure you . . . what a scandal! . . . I heard her voice . . .

(The Poet stands motionlessly across from the doors. The doors open. The Hostess leads the Unknown Woman in.)

HOSTESS. Ladies and gentlemen, a pleasant surprise. My enchanting new acquaintance. I hope we will gladly receive her into our circle of friends. Maria . . . excuse me, I didn't catch your name?
UNKNOWN WOMAN. Maria.
HOSTESS. But . . . your patronymic?
UNKNOWN WOMAN. Maria. I call myself Maria.
HOSTESS. Very well, my dear. I will call you: Mary. There's a certain eccentricity in you, isn't there? But our delightful guest will help us spend this evening that much more happily. Isn't that right, ladies and gentlemen?

(Everyone is confused. An awkward silence. The Host notices that one of the guests has slipped out into the entryway and goes out after him. A voice excusing itself can be heard, along with the words: "I'm not feeling very well." The Poet stands motionlessly.)

HOSTESS. Well then, perhaps our beautiful poet will continue his interrupted reading? Dear Mary, when you arrived, our renowned poet was giving us a recital, . . . a recital.
POET. Forgive me. Allow me to read another time. I'm very sorry.

(No one expresses any dissatisfaction. The Poet walks up to the Hostess, who makes imploring gestures for some time, but soon ceases. The Poet

calmly sits down in the far corner. He looks at the Unknown Woman thoughtfully.*

The maid hands out whatever has been ordered. A guffaw, single words, and whole phrases burst out of the general murmur of voices:

"No, how she danced!" "Just you listen!" "The Russian intelligentsia . . .")

    SOMEONE. (*Especially loudly.*) You'll never get it! You'll never get it!

(Everyone has forgotten about the Poet. He slowly rises from his place. He draws his hand over his forehead. He takes several steps backward and forward across the room. It is apparent from his face that he is trying to remember something with agonizing effort. At the same time the words "Roquefort" and "Camembert" can be heard from out of the general murmur. Suddenly a terribly animated fat man making circular gestures, rushes to the middle of the room with a shout:

"Brie!"

The Poet stops immediately. For a moment, it seems that he has remembered everything. He takes several quick steps in the direction of the Unknown Woman. But the Astronomer, who is coming in from the entryway in a blue dress coat, bars his way.)

    ASTRONOMER. Excuse me for being in my dress coat and for being late. Straight from a conference. I had to give a paper. Astronomy . . .

(Raises a finger upwards.)

    HOST. (*Approaching.*) What do you know, we were just talking about gastronomy too. Nina, dear, isn't it time for supper?
    HOSTESS. (*Rises.*) Ladies and gentlemen, won't you come in!

(Everyone goes out after her. For some time the Unknown Woman, the Poet, and the Astronomer remain in the darkening drawing room. The Poet and the Astronomer stand at the doors, ready to go out. The Unknown Woman lingers in the interior by the dark, half-opened curtain of the window.)

    ASTRONOMER. And so we meet again. I'm very glad. But let the circumstances of our first meeting remain our secret.

POET. I ask the same of you too.
ASTRONOMER. I just gave a paper at the Astronomy society – about what you were an involuntary witness to. A striking fact: a star of the first magnitude . . .
POET. Yes, that's very interesting.
ASTRONOMER. (*Enthusiastically.*) Yes! I entered a new paragraph into my records: "The star Maria has fallen!" For the first time, science . . . Oh, forgive me for not asking you about the results of your search . . .
POET. My search was without result.

(He turns to the interior of the room. He looks around hopelessly. There is languor on his face, emptiness and gloom in his eyes. He staggers from the terrible tension. But he has forgotten everything.)

HOSTESS. (*On the threshold.*) Gentlemen! Come in to the dining room! Where is Mary . . .

(Threatens them with her finger.)

HOSTESS. Oh, you young people! Did you hide my Mary somewhere?

(Looks into the interior of the room.)

HOSTESS. Where is Mary? I say, where is Mary?

(There is no longer anyone by the dark curtain. A bright star shines beyond the window. There falls a blue snow, as blue as the dresscoat of the Astronomer who has disappeared.)

1906

7. Dmitrievsky's lithograph, "On the Bridge", for Blok's play, *The Unknown Woman*, 1922
Courtesy of Union of Theater Workers' Library, Moscow

CONTEXT OF *THE UNKNOWN WOMAN*

RELATED POEMS

THE UNKNOWN WOMAN
In the evenings the ardent air
Over the restaurants is wild and hollow;
A corrupt and vernal spirit
Rules with the shouts of alcoholics.

Beyond, above the crossroad dust,
Above the boredom of suburban dachas,
There glows a baker's gilded pretzel,
And you can hear the children screeching.

And every evening beyond the turnpike,
The tried and tested wits,
Cocking their slanting derbies,
Stroll with their ladies on amongst the ditches.

Above the lake, the locks are creaking,
In the sky, to all inured
though you can hear a woman's shriek,
A disk inanely glowers.

And every evening my only friend
Is reflected in my glass
Like me, he is subdued and stunned
By liquid that is tart, mysterious.

Beside the neighboring tables, close by,
The waiters hang out and "get lost,"
And drunks with rabbit eyes
Cry, "In vino veritas!"

And every evening at the appointed hour
(Or am I only dreaming this?)
Swathed in silks, a woman's figure
Moves in the window laced with mist.

Always without escort, alone,
(The drunks remain where she has passed),
By the window she sits down
Slowly, breathing in perfume and mists.

From her resilient silks there wafts
Ancient knowledge as if winnowed.
Her hat — all plumage and mournful tufts.
Her hand, adorned in rings, is narrow.

Fettered by her estranging nearness,
I look beyond her dark veil's haze,
And make out an enchanted shore
And an enchanted distant space.

Obscure, these mysteries are given in trust
To me, along with someone's sun;
And my soul is pierced in all its twists
And turns by sharp, tart wine.

And in my brain there sway
Those lilting feathers from an ostrich,
And blue, unfathomable eyes
On some distant shore are blossoming.

In my soul there lies a treasure,
With the key to me alone entrusted.
Yes, you are right, you drunken horror!
Now I know: In wine – the Truth.

24 April 1906

THERE, IN THE HARD, HOWLING FROST OF THE NIGHT

There, in the hard, howling frost of the night,
I searched for a ring in a field of stars.
Look, a face arises from out of the lace,
And from out of the lace arises a face.

There her blizzard trills swim,
Dragging bright stars in their train,
And a snowstorm tamborine flies up,
Jingling bells as it beckons.

With a light crackle, her fan goes to pieces, –
Oh, that means not to drink, not to eat![28]
But in her eyes, which are turned to the north,
There is burning news for the cold one – for me.

And twining covers over this moment,
All swathed in the stars of the blizzard,
You swim off to a twilight of snow,
My friend, you, for eons foretold.

August 1905

---

28 As first published in the journal *The Golden Fleece* [*Zolotoe runo*], the poem had a different tenth line: "Opening wide a vengeance of stars . . ."

STAR-STREWN TRAIN

Star-strewn train,
Light blue, blue, blue gaze.
Earth and heaven twain,
A raised bonfire like a blizzard.

Life and death in ever whirl,
All in tight-fit silks,
You are open to the Milky Way,
Hidden in thunder clouds.

Sweltering mists were falling.
Light, go out, go out. Haze, spill . . .
You have passed into my hands a torchbowl
With your narrow, white, strange hand.

I will throw the torchbowl into a blue cupola,
And the Milky Way will spill.
You alone ascend over all this wasteland
To unfurl the train of a comet.

Let touch your silver pleats,
Know, with an indifferent heart,
How sweet my suffer-path,
How easy and serene to perish.

September 1906[29]

---

29 First published under the title "To the Maiden of the Milky Way", which Blok later dropped.

YOUR FACE IS PALER THAN IT WAS

Your face is paler than it was
That day, when I gave the signal,
When, having slackened your pace, you hastened
Your easy fore-evening gait.

To everything obedient – here I stand
By a wall that does not glimmer.
What is the heart? A scroll of wonderworks,
Where passion is combined with grief.[30]

Believe me, both of us knew heaven:
Like a bloody star, you flowed.
I measured your path in sorrow,
When you began to fall.

We knew through an ineffable knowledge
One and the same loft height,
And fell together behind a fog,
Marking a leaning line.

But then I found you, and I met
You at the unillumined gates.
This gaze is no less light
Than it was in the misty heights.

My comet! I have read in luminaries
All of your early story,
And I will know the lying luster of dear
Constellations under black silk.

You complete your path before me.
You walk away into the shadows, just as then.
And the same sky is still behind you,
And like that star, you draw your train.

---

30 As first published, the poem included a stanza after the second stanza that Blok later deleted:

You'll notice me today
And understand our fatal bond.
You'll answer me with a black gaze
And lie with a snake's rustling.

Don't tarry, hiding in dark shadows.
Don't be afraid to recollect and gaze.
Your belt, silver and slender,
Is a Milky Way predestined for a wizard.

March 1906[31]

---

31 First published under the title "To the Unknown Woman". In the second edition of his *Collected Works* (1912), Blok entitled the poem "The Encounter". He later dropped both. In Blok's collection *Earth in Snow* [*Zemlia v snegu*] (1908), an epigraph from the poem "The Unknown Woman" was appended to the poem: "Mute mysteries are entrusted me."

THERE LADIES FLAUNT FASHIONS

There ladies flaunt fashions.
There any schoolboy can act like a wit. –
Above the boredom of the dachas, above the suburbs,
Above the dust of sunny lakes.

There, with its crimson rings,
The sunset, unattainable,
Entices and upsets the summer crowd in vain
Above the dust-laden train stations.

There, where I am so poignantly bored,
Sometimes she comes to me –
Brazenly ravishing,
And condescendingly proud.

Through the stout mugs of beer,
And through the dream of ordinary vanity,
Through a veil covered with spots, appear
Her eyes and delicate features.

Enraptured by my happy star,
Both deafened and upset
By wine, the sunset, and by you,
What is it I await?

Exhaling ancient legends,
Tumultuous in your black silks,
Have you been deafened by the wine
Under your helmet with its funereal plumes?

Amidst this enigmatic vulgarity,
Tell me – what am I to do with you –
As unattainable and singular
As this evening, full of smoke and blue.

April 1906 – 28 April 1911[32]

---

32 First published in Blok's *Collected Poems* (1912) under the title "The Unknown Woman (Variant)".

Printed and bound by PG in the USA